Modern C++ for Absolute Beginners

A Friendly Introduction to the C++ Programming Language and C++11 to C++23 Standards

Second Edition

Slobodan Dmitrović

Apress®

Modern C++ for Absolute Beginners: A Friendly Introduction to the C++ Programming Language and C++11 to C++23 Standards

Slobodan Dmitrović
Belgrade, Serbia

ISBN-13 (pbk): 978-1-4842-9273-0   ISBN-13 (electronic): 978-1-4842-9274-7
https://doi.org/10.1007/978-1-4842-9274-7

Managing Director, Apress Media LLC: Welmoed Spahr
Acquisitions Editor: Steve Anglin
Development Editor: James Markham
Coordinating Editor: Gryffin Winkler

Cover image designed by eStudioCalamar

Distributed to the book trade worldwide by Springer Science+Business Media New York, 1 New York Plaza, Suite 4600, New York, NY 10004-1562, USA. Phone 1-800-SPRINGER, fax (201) 348-4505, e-mail orders-ny@ springer-sbm.com, or visit www.springeronline.com. Apress Media, LLC is a California LLC and the sole member (owner) is Springer Science + Business Media Finance Inc (SSBM Finance Inc). SSBM Finance Inc is a **Delaware** corporation.

For information on translations, please e-mail booktranslations@springernature.com; for reprint, paperback, or audio rights, please e-mail bookpermissions@springernature.com.

Apress titles may be purchased in bulk for academic, corporate, or promotional use. eBook versions and licenses are also available for most titles. For more information, reference our Print and eBook Bulk Sales web page at http://www.apress.com/bulk-sales.

Any source code or other supplementary material referenced by the author in this book is available to readers on GitHub via the book's product page, located at www.apress.com/. For more detailed information, please visit http://www.apress.com/source-code.

Printed on acid-free paper

To Mary Anne,
whose work is an inspiration to me.

Table of Contents

About the Author

 **Slobodan Dmitrović** is a software consultant, trainer, and author of several programming books. He is a professional R&D software developer with two decades of experience in the industry. Slobodan provides C++ training courses for corporate clients and academic institutions. Connect with Slobodan at `https://www.linkedin.com/in/slobodan-dmitrovic/`.

About the Technical Reviewer

Germán González-Morris is a polyglot software architect/engineer with 20+ years of experience in the field, having knowledge in Java, Spring, C, Julia, Python, Haskell, and JavaScript, among others. He works for cloud (architecture) and web distributed applications. Germán loves math puzzles (including reading Knuth), swimming, and table tennis. Also, he has reviewed several books including an application container book (WebLogic) and books on languages (C, Haskell, TypeScript, WebAssembly, Math for coders, regexp, Julia, Algorithms). For more details, you can visit his blog (https://devwebcl.blogspot.com/) or Twitter account (@devwebcl).

Acknowledgments

I want to thank my friends, readers, and fellow C++ peers who have supported me in writing the second edition of this book.

I am thankful to the entire C++ community for their help and feedback. I would like to thank Rainer Grimm, Klaus Iglberger, Jens Weller, Bartłomiej Filipek, and many others.

My most profound appreciation goes to S. Antonijević, Ron and Brankica, and Saša Popović for their ongoing support.

About the Second Edition

The second edition of this book is updated to include the notable features inside the C++23 standard.

I have revised and updated numerous chapters with more relevant information and clarification.

The second edition includes more diagrams to represent certain concepts better.

I have also added the output for all the code snippets.

The book now has a chapter entirely dedicated to various projects.

My intent with the second edition was to provide a simplified, updated, and accurate introduction to the modern C++ programming language.

CHAPTER 1

Introduction

Congratulations on choosing to learn the C++ programming language, and thank you for picking up this book. I will try to introduce you to a beautiful world of C++ to the best of my abilities.

This book is an effort to introduce the reader to the C++ programming language in a structured, straightforward, and friendly manner. We will use the "just enough theory and plenty of examples" approach whenever possible.

To me, C++ is a wonderful product of the human intellect. Over the years, I have certainly come to think of it as a thing of beauty and elegance. C++ is a language like no other, surprising in its complexity yet wonderfully sleek and elegant in so many ways. It is also a language that cannot be learned by guessing, one that is easy to get wrong and challenging to get right.

In this book, we will get familiar with the language basics first. Then, we will move on to classes, templates, and the C++ Standard Library. Once we got these covered, we will describe the modern C++ standards in more detail.

After each section, source code exercises will help us adopt the learned material more efficiently.

Finally, we will create a couple of source code projects. Let us get started!

© Slobodan Dmitrović 2023
S. Dmitrović, *Modern C++ for Absolute Beginners*, https://doi.org/10.1007/978-1-4842-9274-7_1

CHAPTER 2

What Is C++?

C++ is a programming language – a standardized, general-purpose, object-oriented, compiled language. Every C++ compiler is accompanied by a set of useful functions and containers called the C++ Standard Library. Bjarne Stroustrup created C++ as an extension to a C programming language. Still, C++ evolved to be a completely different programming language.

Let us emphasize this: C and C++ are two different languages. C++ started as "C with classes," but it is now a completely different language. So, C++ is not C; C++ is not C with classes; it is just C++. And there is no such thing as a C/C++ programming language.

C++ is widely used for so-called systems programming as well as application programming. C++ is a language that allows us to *get down to the metal* where we can perform low-level routines if needed or soar high using abstraction mechanisms such as templates and classes.

C++ Standards

C++ is governed by the ISO C++ standard. There are multiple ISO C++ standards listed here in chronological order: C++03, C++11, C++14, C++17, C++20, and the upcoming C++23 standard.

Every C++ standard, starting with C++11 onward, is referred to as "modern C++." And modern C++ is what we will be teaching in this book.

© Slobodan Dmitrović 2023
S. Dmitrović, *Modern C++ for Absolute Beginners*, https://doi.org/10.1007/978-1-4842-9274-7_2

CHAPTER 3

C++ Compilers

C++ programs are usually a collection of some C++ code spread across one or multiple source and header files. Source files, by convention, have the .cpp extension, and header files, by convention, have the .h extension. Other extensions are also possible. Both header and source files are regular text files containing some C++ source code. The C++ compiler is a program that compiles these files and turns them into object files. A linker then links object files together to create an executable file or a library. At the time of writing, some of the more popular C++ compilers are

- The g++ front end (as part of the GNU Compiler Collection or GCC)

- Visual C++ (as part of the Visual Studio IDE)

- Clang (as part of the LLVM)

Installing C++ Compilers

The following sections explain how to install C++ compilers on Linux and Windows and compile and run our C++ programs.

On Linux

To install a C++ compiler (as part of the GCC) on Linux Ubuntu, type the following inside the terminal:

```
sudo apt-get install build-essential
```

To install a C++ compiler on Fedora, we type

```
sudo dnf install gcc-c++
```

5

© Slobodan Dmitrović 2023
S. Dmitrović, *Modern C++ for Absolute Beginners*, https://doi.org/10.1007/978-1-4842-9274-7_3

To compile the C++ source file, named, for example, **source.cpp**, we type

```
g++ source.cpp
```

This command will produce an executable with the default name of **a.out**. To run the executable file, type

```
./a.out
```

To compile for a C++11 standard, we add the -std=c++11 flag:

```
g++ -std=c++11 source.cpp
```

To enable warnings, we add the *-Wall* flag:

```
g++ -std=c++11 -Wall source.cpp
```

To produce a custom executable name, we add the *-o* flag followed by an executable name:

```
g++ -std=c++11 -Wall source.cpp -o myexe
```

Alternatively, we can install a Clang compiler on Linux Ubuntu by typing

```
sudo apt-get install clang
```

To install Clang on Fedora, we type

```
sudo dnf install clang
```

The same rules apply to the Clang compiler when compiling. Substitute *g*++ with *clang*++.

On Windows

On Windows, we can install a free or commercial copy of Visual Studio.

Choose *Create a new project,* make sure the *C++* language option is selected, choose *Empty Project*, click *Next*, and click *Create*. Go to the Solution Explorer panel, right-click the project name, choose *Add ➤ New Item ➤ C++ File (.cpp)*, type the name of a file (**source.cpp**), and click *Add*. Press F5 to run the program.

We can also do the following: choose *Create a new project*, make sure the *C++* language option is selected, choose *Console App,* click *Next,* and click *Create*.

If a *Create a new project* button is not visible, choose *File ➤ New ➤ Project* and repeat the remaining steps.

CHAPTER 4

Our First Program

Let us create a blank text file using the text editor or C++ IDE of our choice and name it *source.cpp*. First, let us create an empty C++ program that does nothing. The content of the *source.cpp* file is

```cpp
int main(){}
```

The function `main` is the main program's entry point, the start of our program. When we run our executable, the code inside the `main` function body gets executed. A function is of type `int` (and returns a result to the system, but let us not worry about that just yet). The reserved name `main` is a function name. It is followed by a list of parameters inside the parentheses () followed by a function body marked with braces {}. Braces marking the beginning and the end of a function body can also be on separate lines:

```cpp
int main()
{
}
```

This simple program does nothing, it has no parameters listed inside parentheses, and there are no statements inside the function body. It is essential to understand that this is the main program signature.

There is also another `main` function signature accepting two different parameters used for manipulating the command-line arguments. For now, we will only use the first form.

Comments

Single-line comments in C++ start with double slashes //, and the compiler ignores them. We use them to comment or document the code or use them as notes:

```cpp
int main()
{
```

7

© Slobodan Dmitrović 2023
S. Dmitrović, *Modern C++ for Absolute Beginners*, https://doi.org/10.1007/978-1-4842-9274-7_4

```
    // this is a comment
}
```

We can have multiple single-line comments:

```
int main()
{
    // this is a comment
    // this is another comment
}
```

Multiline comments start with the /* and end with the */. They are also known as C-style comments. Example:

```
int main()
{
    /* This is a
    multi-line comment */
}
```

Hello World Example

Now we are ready to get the first glimpse at our "Hello World" example. The following program is the simplest "Hello World" example. It prints out "Hello World." in the console window:

```
#include <iostream>

int main()
{
    std::cout << "Hello World.";
}
```

Output:

___

```
Hello World.
```

___

Believe it or not, this example's detailed analysis and explanation can be more than 15 pages long. We can go into it right now, but we will be no wiser at this point as we first need to know what headers, streams, objects, operators, and string literals are. Do not worry. We will get there.

Explanation:

The #include <iostream> statement includes the iostream header file content into our source file via the #include directive. The iostream header is part of the standard library. We need its inclusion to be able to use the std::cout object, also known as the *standard output stream.* The << operator, called the *stream insertion operator,* inserts our Hello World string literal into that output stream. A string literal is enclosed in double quotes "". The ; marks the end of the statement. Statements are pieces of the C++ program that get executed. Statements end with a semicolon ; in C++. The std is the standard library namespace, and :: is the *scope resolution operator.* Object cout is located inside the std namespace, and to access it, we need to prepend the call with the std::. We will get more familiar with all of these later in the book, especially the std:: part.

A brief explanation:

In a nutshell, the std::cout << is the natural way of outputting data to the standard output/console window in C++.

We can output multiple string literals by separating them with multiple << operators:

```
#include <iostream>

int main()
{
    std::cout << "Some string." << " Another string.";
}
```

Output:

```
Some string. Another string.
```

To output data on a new line, we need to output a newline character \n literal. A single character literal, including the escape sequence characters in C++, is enclosed in single quotes '', like 'a', 'B', 'c', '\n', etc.

Example:

```
#include <iostream>

int main()
{
    std::cout << "First line" << '\n' << "Second line.";
}
```

Output:

```
First line
Second line.
```

Certain characters cannot be easily represented using a single character symbol. Some character literals start with the \ symbol. The \ represents an *escape sequence,* a mechanism to represent certain special characters such as the *newline character* '\n', a *single quote character* '\'', a *double quote character* '\"', a character '\t', and similar.

Characters can also be part of the single string literal:

```
#include <iostream>

int main()
{
    std::cout << "First line\nSecond line.";
}
```

Output:

```
First line
Second line.
```

Do not use using namespace std;

Many examples on the Web introduce the entire std namespace into the current scope via the using namespace std; statement only to be able to type cout instead of the std::cout. While this might save us from typing five additional characters, it is **wrong** for many reasons. We do not want to introduce the entire *std* namespace into the current scope because we want to avoid name clashes and ambiguity.

Good to remember   Do not introduce the entire std namespace into a current scope via the using namespace std; statement.

So, instead of this wrong approach:

```
#include <iostream>

using namespace std; // do not use this

int main()
{
    cout << "Bad practice.";
}
```

Use the following:

```
#include <iostream>

int main()
{
    std::cout << "Good practice.";
}
```

For calls to objects and functions residing inside the std namespace, add the std:: prefix where needed.

CHAPTER 5

Types

Every entity has a type. What is a type? A type is a property describing the set of possible values and operations on those values. Instances of types are called objects. An object is a region in memory that has a type, a value, and possibly a name. An instance of a simple type is not to be confused with an instance of a class which is also called an object.

Fundamental Types

C++ has some built-in types. We often refer to them as *fundamental types*. A declaration is a statement that introduces a name into a current scope.

Boolean

Let us declare a variable b of type `bool`. This type holds values of `true` and `false`:

```cpp
int main()
{
    bool b;
}
```

This example declares a variable b of type `bool`. And that is it. The variable is not initialized: and no value has been assigned to it at the time of construction. To initialize a variable, we use an assignment operator = followed by an initializer:

```cpp
int main()
{
    bool b = true;
}
```

© Slobodan Dmitrović 2023
S. Dmitrović, *Modern C++ for Absolute Beginners*, https://doi.org/10.1007/978-1-4842-9274-7_5

We can also use braces {} for initialization:

```
int main()
{
    bool b{ true };
}
```

These examples declare a (local) variable b of type bool and initialize it to a value of true. Our variable now holds a value of true. All local variables should be initialized. Accessing uninitialized variables results in undefined behavior, abbreviated as UB. More on this in the following chapters.

Character Type

Type char, referred to as *character type,* is used to represent a single character. The type can store characters such as 'a', 'Z', etc. The size of a character type is exactly one byte. Character literals are enclosed in single quotes ' ' in C++. To declare and initialize a variable of type char, we write

```
int main()
{
    char c = 'a';
}
```

Now we can print out the value of our char variable:

```
#include <iostream>

int main()
{
    char c = 'a';
    std::cout << "The value of variable c is: " << c;
}
```

Output:

```
The value of variable c is: a
```

Once declared and initialized, we can access our variable and change its value:

```cpp
#include <iostream>

int main()
{
    char c = 'a';
    std::cout << "The value of variable c is: " << c;
    c = 'B';
    std::cout << " The new value of variable c is: " << c;
}
```

Output:

```
The value of variable c is: a The new value of variable c is: B
```

The size of the char type in memory is always one byte. We obtain the size of the type through a sizeof operator:

```cpp
#include <iostream>

int main()
{
    std::cout << "The size of type char is: " << sizeof(char) << "
    byte(s)";
}
```

Output:

```
The size of type char is: 1 byte(s)
```

There are other character types, such as wchar_t for holding characters of Unicode character set and char16_t for holding UTF-16 character sets, but for now, let us stick to the type char.

A character literal is a character enclosed in single quotes, for example, 'a', 'A', 'z', 'X', 'o', etc.

Every character is represented by an integer number in the character set. That is why we can assign both numeric literals (up to a certain number) and character literals to our char variable:

```
int main()
{
    char c = 'a';
    // is the same as:
    // char c = 97;
}
```

We can write char c = 'a'; or we can write char c = 97; which is (probably) the same, as the 'a' character in the ASCII table is represented with the number of 97. For the most part, we will be using character literals to represent the value of a char object.

Integer Types

Another fundamental type is int called integer type. We use it to store integral values (whole numbers), both negative and positive:

```
#include <iostream>

int main()
{
    int x = 123;
    int y = -256;
    std::cout << "The value of x is: " << x << ", the value of y
    is: " << y;
}
```

Output:

```
The value of x is: 123, the value of y is: -256
```

Here, we declared and initialized two variables of type int. The size of int is usually 4 bytes. We can also initialize the variable with another variable. It will receive a copy of its value. We still have two separate objects in memory:

```cpp
#include <iostream>

int main()
{
    int x = 123;
    int y = x;
    std::cout << "The value of x is: " << x << ", the value of y
    is: " << y;
    // x is 123
    // y is 123
    x = 456;
    std::cout << "The value of x is: " << x << ", the value of y
    is: " << y;
    // x is now 456
    // y is still 123
}
```

Output:

```
The value of x is: 123, the value of y is: 123The value of x is: 456, the
value of y is: 123
```

Once we declare a variable, we access and manipulate the variable name by its name only, without the type name.

Integer literals can be decimal, octal, and hexadecimal. Octal literals start with a prefix of 0, and hexadecimal literals begin with a prefix of 0x.

```cpp
int main()
{
    int x = 10;      // decimal literal
    int y = 012;     // octal literal
    int z = 0xA;     // hexadecimal literal
}
```

All these variables have been initialized to a value of 10 represented by different integer literals. For the most part, we will be using decimal literals.

There are also other integer types, such as int64_t and others, but we will stick to int for now.

Floating-Point Types

There are three floating-point types in C++: float, double, and long double. Mainly, we will be using the type double (double precision). We use it for storing floating-point values/real numbers:

```
#include <iostream>

int main()
{
    double d = 3.14;
    std::cout << "The value of d is: " << d;
}
```

Output:

```
The value of d is: 3.14
```

Some of the floating-point literals can be

```
int main()
{
    double x = 213.456;
    double y = 1.;
    double z = 0.15;
    double w = .15;
    double d = 3.14e10;
}
```

Type void

Type void is a type with no values. Well, what is the purpose of such a type if we cannot have objects of that type? Good question. While we cannot have objects of type void, we can have functions of type void – functions that do not return a value. We can also have a void pointer type marked with void*. More on this in later chapters when we discuss pointers and functions.

Type Modifiers

Types can have modifiers. Some of the modifiers are signed and unsigned. The signed (the default if omitted) means the type can hold both positive and negative values, and unsigned means the type has unsigned representation. Other modifiers affect the type's size: short means the type will have a width of at least 16 bits, and long means the type will have a width of at least 32 bits. Furthermore, we can now combine these modifiers:

```cpp
#include <iostream>

int main()
{
    unsigned long int x = 4294967295;
    std::cout << "The value of an unsigned long integer variable
    is: " << x;
}
```

Output:

```
The value of an unsigned long integer variable is: 4294967295
```

Type int is signed by default.

Variable Declaration, Definition, and Initialization

Introducing a name into a current scope is called a *declaration*. We are letting the world know there is a name (a variable, for example) of some type from now on in the current scope. In a declaration, we prepend the variable name with a type name. Declaration examples:

```cpp
int main()
{
    char c;
    int x;
    double d;
}
```

We can declare multiple names on the same line:

```
int main()
{
    int x, y, z;
}
```

If there is an initializer for an object present, then we call it an *initialization*. We are declaring and initializing an object to a specific value. We can initialize an object in various ways:

```
int main()
{
    int x = 123;
    int y{ 123 };
    int z = { 123 };
}
```

A variable definition is setting a value in memory for a name. The definition is making sure we can access and use the name in our program. Roughly speaking, it is a declaration followed by an initialization (for variables) followed by a semicolon. The definition is also a declaration. Definition examples:

```
int main()
{
    char c = 'a';
    int x = 123;
    double d = 456.78;
}
```

CHAPTER 6

Exercises

Hello World and Comments

Write a program that has a comment in it and outputs "Hello World." on one line and "C++ rocks!" on a new line.

```cpp
#include <iostream>

int main()
{
    // this is a comment
    std::cout << "Hello World." << '\n';
    std::cout << "C++ rocks!";
}
```

Output:

```
Hello World.
C++ rocks!
```

Declaration

Write a program that declares three variables inside the main function. Variables are of types char, int, and double. The names of the variables are arbitrary. Since we do not use any input or output, we do not need to include the <iostream> header.

```cpp
int main()
{
    char mychar;
```

© Slobodan Dmitrović 2023
S. Dmitrović, *Modern C++ for Absolute Beginners*, https://doi.org/10.1007/978-1-4842-9274-7_6

```
    int myint;
    double mydouble;
}
```

Definition

Write a program that defines three variables inside the `main` function. The variables are of types `char`, `int`, and `double`. The names of the variables are arbitrary. The initializers are arbitrary.

```
int main()
{
    char mychar = 'a';
    int myint = 123;
    double mydouble = 456.78;
}
```

Initialization

Write a program that defines three variables inside the `main` function. The variables are of types `char`, `int`, and `double`. The names of the variables are arbitrary. The initializers are arbitrary. The initialization is performed using the initializer list. Print the values afterward.

```
#include <iostream>

int main()
{
    char mychar{ 'a' };
    int myint{ 123 };
    double mydouble{ 456.78 };
    std::cout << "The value of a char variable is: " << mychar << '\n';
    std::cout << "The value of an int variable is: " << myint << '\n';
    std::cout << "The value of a double variable is: " << mydouble << '\n';
}
```

Output:

```
The value of a char variable is: a
The value of an int variable is: 123
The value of a double variable is: 456.78
```

CHAPTER 7

Operators

Assignment Operator

The assignment operator = assigns a value to a variable/object:

```
int main()
{
    char mychar = 'c';    // define a char variable mychar
    mychar = 'd';         // assign a new value to mychar
    int x = 123;          // define an integer variable x
    x = 456;              // assign a new value to x
    int y = 789;          // define a new integer variable y
    y = x;                // assign a value of x to it
}
```

Arithmetic Operators

We can do arithmetic operations using arithmetic operators. Some of them are

```
+ // addition
- // subtraction
* // multiplication
/ // division
% // modulo
```

Example:

```
#include <iostream>

int main()
```

© Slobodan Dmitrović 2023
S. Dmitrović, *Modern C++ for Absolute Beginners*, https://doi.org/10.1007/978-1-4842-9274-7_7

```cpp
{
    int x = 123;
    int y = 456;
    int result = x + y; // addition
    result = x - y; // subtraction
    result = x * y; // multiplication
    result = x / y; // division
    std::cout << "The result is: " << result << '\n';
}
```

Output:

```
The result is: 0
```

The integer division, in our example, results in a value of 0. It is because the result of the integral division where both operands are integers is *truncated toward zeros*. In the expression x / y, x and y are operands, and / is the operator.

If we want a floating-point result, we need to use the type double and make sure at least one of the division operands is also of type double:

```cpp
#include <iostream>

int main()
{
    int x = 123;
    double y = 456.0;
    double result = x / y;
    std::cout << "The division result is: " << result << '\n';
}
```

Output:

```
The division result is: 0.269737
```

Similarly, we can have

```cpp
#include <iostream>

int main()
```

26

```
{
    double result = 123 / 456.0;
    std::cout << "The division result is: " << result << '\n';
}
```

Output:

```
The division result is: 0.269737
```

And the result would be the same as in the previous example.

Compound Assignment Operators

Compound assignment operators allow us to perform an arithmetic operation and assign a result with one operator:

```
+= // compound addition
-= // compound subtraction
*= // compound multiplication
/= // compound division
%= // compound modulo
```

Example:

```
#include <iostream>

int main()
{
    int x = 123;
    x += 10;    // the same as x = x + 10
    x -= 10;    // the same as x = x - 10
    x *= 2;     // the same as x = x * 2
    x /= 3;     // the same as x = x / 3
    std::cout << "The value of x is: " << x;
}
```

Output:

```
The value of x is: 82
```

Increment/Decrement Operators

Increment/decrement operators increment/decrement the value of the object. The operators are

```
++x // pre-increment operator
x++ // post-increment operator
--x // pre-decrement operator
x-- // post-decrement operator
```

Here's a simple example:

```cpp
#include <iostream>

int main()
{
    int x = 123;
    x++;    // add 1 to the value of x
    ++x;    // add 1 to the value of x
    --x;    // decrement the value of x by 1
    x--;    // decrement the value of x by 1
    std::cout << "The value of x is: " << x;
}
```

Output:

```
The value of x is: 123
```

Both preincrement and postincrement operators add 1 to the value of our object, and both predecrement and postdecrement operators subtract one from the value of our object. The difference between the two, apart from the implementation mechanism, is that with the preincrement operator, a value of 1 is added first, and then the variable/object is evaluated/accessed in the expression. With the postincrement, the object is evaluated/accessed first, and after that, the value of 1 is added. To the next statement that follows, it does not make a difference. The value of the object is the same, no matter what version of the operator was used. The only difference is the timing in the expression where it is used.

CHAPTER 8

Standard Input

C++ provides facilities for accepting input from a user. We can think of the *standard input* as our keyboard. A simple example of accepting one integer number and printing it out is

```cpp
#include <iostream>

int main()
{
    std::cout << "Please enter a number and press enter: ";
    int x = 0;
    std::cin >> x;
    std::cout << "You entered: " << x;
}
```

Possible Output:

```
Please enter a number and press enter: 123
You entered: 123
```

The std::cin is the standard input stream, and it uses the *stream extraction* >> operator to extract what has been read into our variable. The std::cin >> x; statement means *read from standard input into a variable x*. The cin object resides inside the std namespace. So, std::cout << is used for outputting data (to a screen), and std::cin >> is used for inputting the data (from the keyboard).

We can accept multiple values from the standard input by separating them with multiple >> operators:

```cpp
#include <iostream>

int main()
{
```

© Slobodan Dmitrović 2023
S. Dmitrović, *Modern C++ for Absolute Beginners*, https://doi.org/10.1007/978-1-4842-9274-7_8

```
    std::cout << "Please enter two numbers separated by a space and press
    enter: ";
    int x = 0;
    int y = 0;
    std::cin >> x >> y;
    std::cout << "You entered: " << x << " and " << y;
}
```

Possible Output:

```
Please enter two numbers separated by a space and press enter: 123 456
You entered: 123 and 456
```

We can accept values of different types:

```
#include <iostream>

int main()
{
    std::cout << "Please enter a character, an integer, and a double: ";
    char c = 0;
    int x = 0;
    double d = 0.0;
    std::cin >> c >> x >> d;
    std::cout << "You entered: " << c << ", " << x << " and " << d;
}
```

Possible Output:

```
Please enter a character, an integer, and a double: A 123 3.14
You entered: A, 123 and 3.14
```

CHAPTER 9

Exercises

Standard Input

Write a program that accepts an integer number from the standard input and then prints it out.

```
#include <iostream>

int main()
{
    std::cout << "Please enter a number: ";
    int x;
    std::cin >> x;
    std::cout << "You entered: " << x;
}
```

Possible Output:

```
Please enter a number: 123
You entered: 123
```

Two Inputs

Write a program that accepts two integer numbers from the standard input and then prints them out.

```
#include <iostream>

int main()
{
```

© Slobodan Dmitrović 2023
S. Dmitrović, *Modern C++ for Absolute Beginners*, https://doi.org/10.1007/978-1-4842-9274-7_9

```
    std::cout << "Please enter two integer numbers: ";
    int x;
    int y;
    std::cin >> x >> y;
    std::cout << "You entered: " << x << " and " << y;
}
```

Possible Output:

```
Please enter two integer numbers: 123 456
You entered: 123 and 456
```

Multiple Inputs

Write a program that accepts three values of type char, int, and double respectively from the standard input. Print out the values afterward.

```
#include <iostream>

int main()
{
    std::cout << "Please enter a char, an int, and a double: ";
    char c;
    int x;
    double d;
    std::cin >> c >> x >> d;
    std::cout << "You entered: " << c << ", " << x << ", and " << d;
}
```

Possible Output:

```
Please enter a char, an int, and a double: A 123 456.789
You entered: A, 123, and 456.789
```

Inputs and Arithmetic Operations

Write a program that accepts two int numbers, sums them up, and assigns a result to a third integer. Print out the result afterward.

```cpp
#include <iostream>

int main()
{
    std::cout << "Please enter two integer numbers: ";
    int x;
    int y;
    std::cin >> x >> y;
    int result = x + y;
    std::cout << "The result is: " << result;
}
```

Possible Output:

```
Please enter two integer numbers: 10 20
The result is: 30
```

Postincrement and Compound Assignment

Write a program that defines an int variable called x with a value of 100, postincrements that value in the next statement, and adds the value of 10 in the following statement using the compound assignment operator. Print out the value afterward.

```cpp
#include <iostream>

int main()
{
    int x = 100;
    x++;
    x += 10;
    std::cout << "The result is: " << x;
}
```

Output:

The result is: 111

Integral and Floating-Point Division

Write a program that divides numbers 9 and 2 and assigns a result to an int and a double variable. Then modify one of the operands so that it is of type double and observe the different outcomes of a floating-point division where at least one of the operands is of type double. Print out the values afterward.

```cpp
#include <iostream>

int main()
{
    int x = 9 / 2;
    std::cout << "The result is: " << x << '\n';
    double d = 9 / 2;
    std::cout << "The result is: " << d << '\n';
    d = 9.0 / 2;
    std::cout << "The result is: " << d;
}
```

Output:

The result is: 4
The result is: 4
The result is: 4.5

CHAPTER 10

Arrays

Arrays are sequences of objects of the same type. We can declare an array of type char as follows:

```
int main()
{
    char arr[5];
}
```

This example declares an array of five characters. To declare an array of type int, which holds five elements, we would use

```
int main()
{
    int arr[5];
}
```

To initialize an array, we can use the initialization list {}:

```
int main()
{
    int arr[5] = { 10, 20, 30, 40, 50 };
}
```

The initialization list in our example { 10, 20, 30, 40, 50 } is marked with braces and comma-separated values. This initialization list initializes our array with the values in the list. The first array element will be initialized with a value of 10; the second array element will be initialized with a value of 20; etc. The last (fifth) array element now has a value of 50.

We can access individual array elements through a subscript [ ] operator and an index. The first array element has an index of 0, and we access it via

© Slobodan Dmitrović 2023
S. Dmitrović, *Modern C++ for Absolute Beginners*, https://doi.org/10.1007/978-1-4842-9274-7_10

```
int main()
{
    int arr[5] = { 10, 20, 30, 40, 50 };
    arr[0] = 100; // change the value of the first array element
}
```

Since the indexing starts from 0 and not 1, the last array element has an index of 4:

```
int main()
{
    int arr[5] = { 10, 20, 30, 40, 50 };
    arr[4] = 500; // change the value of the last array element
}
```

So, when declaring an array, we write how many elements we want to declare, but when accessing array elements, we need to remember that the indexing starts from 0 and ends with the *number of elements – 1*. That being said, in modern C++, we should prefer the std::array and std::vector containers to raw arrays. More on this in later chapters.

CHAPTER 11

Pointers

Objects reside in memory. And so far, we have learned how to access and manipulate objects through *variables*. Another way to access an object in memory is through pointers. Each object in memory occupies a certain amount of bytes and has a type and an address. This allows us to access the object through a pointer. So, pointers are types that can hold the address of a particular object. For illustrative purposes only, we will declare an unutilized pointer that can point to an `int` object:

```cpp
int main()
{
    int* p;
}
```

We say that p is of type `int*`.

To declare a pointer that points to a `char` (object), we declare a pointer of type `char*`:

```cpp
int main()
{
    char* p;
}
```

In our first example, we declared a pointer of type `int*`. To make it point to an existing `int` object in memory, we use the address-of operator `&`. We say that p *points to* x.

```cpp
int main()
{
    int x = 123;
    int* p = &x;
}
```

In our second example, we declared a pointer of type `char*`, and similarly, we have

© Slobodan Dmitrović 2023
S. Dmitrović, *Modern C++ for Absolute Beginners*, https://doi.org/10.1007/978-1-4842-9274-7_11

```
int main()
{
    char c = 'a';
    char* p = &c;
}
```

To initialize a pointer that does not point to any object, we can use the `nullptr` literal:

```
int main()
{
    char* p = nullptr;
}
```

It is said that p is now a *null pointer*.

Pointers are variables/objects, just like any other type of object. Their value is the address of an object, a memory location where the object is stored. To access a value stored in an object pointed to by a pointer, we need to *dereference a pointer*. Dereferencing is done by prepending a pointer (variable) name with a dereferencing operator *:

```
int main()
{
    char c = 'a';
    char* p = &c;
    char d = *p;
}
```

To print out the value of the dereferenced pointer, we can use the following:

```
#include <iostream>

int main()
{
    char c = 'a';
    char* p = &c;
    std::cout << "The value of the dereferenced pointer is: " << *p;
}
```

Output:

```
The value of the dereferenced pointer is: a
```

Now, the value of the dereferenced pointer *p is simply 'a'.

Similarly, for an integer pointer, we would have

```cpp
#include <iostream>

int main()
{
    int x = 123;
    int* p = &x;
    std::cout << "The value of the dereferenced pointer is: " << *p;
}
```

Output:

```
The value of the dereferenced pointer is: 123
```

And the value of the dereferenced pointer, in this case, would be 123.

We can change the value of the pointed-to object through a dereferenced pointer:

```cpp
#include <iostream>

int main()
{
    int x = 123;
    int* p = &x;
    *p = 456; // change the value of pointed-to object
    std::cout << "The value of x is: " << x;
}
```

Output:

```
The value of x is: 456
```

We will talk about pointers, and especially about **smart pointers**, when we cover the concepts such as dynamic memory allocation and the lifetime of an object.

CHAPTER 12

References

Another (somewhat) similar concept is a *reference type*. A reference type is *an alias to an existing object in memory*. References must be initialized. We describe a reference type as type_name followed by an ampersand &. Example:

```
int main()
{
    int x = 123;
    int& y = x;
}
```

Now we have two different names that refer to the same int object in memory. We can visualize the object in memory using the following image:

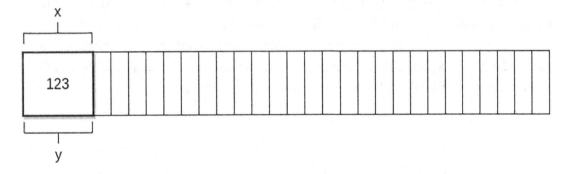

If we assign a different value to either one of them, the object's value will change as we have one object in memory, but we are using two different names:

```
int main()
{
    int x = 123;
    int& y = x;
```

© Slobodan Dmitrović 2023
S. Dmitrović, *Modern C++ for Absolute Beginners*, https://doi.org/10.1007/978-1-4842-9274-7_12

```
    x = 456;
    // both x and y now hold the value of 456
    y = 789;
    // both x and y now hold the value of 789
}
```

Another concept is a `const` reference, a read-only alias to some object. Example:

```
int main()
{
    int x = 123;
    const int& y = x; // const reference
    x = 456;
    // both x and y now hold the value of 456
}
```

We will discuss references and `const` reference in more detail when we learn about functions and function parameters. For now, let us assume they are an alias, a different/ additional name we give to our existing object.

It is important not to confuse the use of * in a pointer type declaration such as `int* p;` and the use of * when dereferencing a pointer such as `*p = 456`. Although the same star character, it is used in two different contexts.

It is important not to confuse the use of ampersand & in reference type declaration such as `int& y = x;` and the use of ampersand as an address-of operator such as `int* p = &x`. The same literal symbol is used for two different things.

CHAPTER 13

Introduction to Strings

Earlier, we mentioned printing out a string literal such as `"Hello World."` to a standard output via:

```
std::cout << "Hello World.";
```

We can store these string literals inside a `std::string` type. The C++ Standard Library offers a compound type called `string` or rather `std::string` as it is part of the `std` namespace. We use it for storing and manipulating strings.

Defining a String

To use the `std::string` type, we need to include the `<string>` header in our program:

```
#include <string>

int main()
{
    std::string s = "Hello World.";
}
```

To print out this string on the standard output, we use

```
#include <iostream>
#include <string>

int main()
{
    std::string s = "Hello World.";
    std::cout << s;
}
```

© Slobodan Dmitrović 2023

S. Dmitrović, *Modern C++ for Absolute Beginners*, https://doi.org/10.1007/978-1-4842-9274-7_13

Output:

```
Hello World.
```

Concatenating Strings

We can add a string literal to our string using the compound operator +=:

```cpp
#include <iostream>
#include <string>

int main()
{
    std::string s = "Hello ";
    s += "World.";
    std::cout << s;
}
```

Output:

```
Hello World.
```

We can add a character to our string using the += operator:

```cpp
#include <iostream>
#include <string>

int main()
{
    std::string s = "Hello";
    char c = '!';
    s += c;
    std::cout << s;
}
```

Output:

```
Hello!
```

We can add another string to our string using the + operator. We say we *concatenate* the strings:

```cpp
#include <iostream>
#include <string>

int main()
{
    std::string s1 = "Hello ";
    std::string s2 = "World.";
    std::string s3 = s1 + s2;
    std::cout << s3;
}
```

Output:

```
Hello World.
```

Internally, the type `std::string` is the so-called *class template*. It is implemented using templates, which we will discuss later on. For now, we will just mention that this string class offers some functionality (member functions) for working with strings.

Accessing Characters

Individual characters of a string can be accessed through a subscript operator [ ] or via a member function *.at(index)*. The index starts at 0. Example:

```cpp
#include <iostream>
#include <string>

int main()
{
    std::string s = "Hello World.";
    char c1 = s[0];         // 'H'
    char c2 = s.at(0);      // 'H';
    char c3 = s[6];         // 'W'
```

```
    char c4 = s.at(6);      // 'W';
    std::cout << "First character: " << c1 << ", sixth character: " << c3;
}
```

Output:

```
First character: H, sixth character: W
```

Comparing Strings

A string can be compared to string literals and other strings using the equality ==
operator. Comparing a string to a string literal:

```
#include <iostream>
#include <string>

int main()
{
    std::string s1 = "Hello";
    if (s1 == "Hello")
    {
        std::cout << "The string is equal to \"Hello\"";
    }
}
```

Output:

```
The string is equal to "Hello"
```

Comparing a string to another string is done using the equality operator ==:

```
#include <iostream>
#include <string>

int main()
{
    std::string s1 = "Hello";
    std::string s2 = "World.";
```

```
    if (s1 == s2)
    {
        std::cout << "The strings are equal.";
    }
    else
    {
        std::cout << "The strings are not equal.";
    }
}
```

Output:

```
The strings are not equal.
```

String Input

The preferred way of accepting a string from the standard input is via the `std::getline` function, which takes `std::cin` and our string as parameters:

```
#include <iostream>
#include <string>

int main()
{
    std::string s;
    std::cout << "Please enter a string: ";
    std::getline(std::cin, s);
    std::cout << "You entered: " << s;
}
```

Possible Output:

```
Please enter a string: Sample string.
You entered: Sample string.
```

We use the `std::getline` because our string can contain white spaces. And if we used the `std::cin` function alone, it would accept only a part of the string.

The `std::getline` function has the following signature: `std::getline(read_from, into);`. The function reads a line of text from the standard input (`std::cin`) into a string (`s`) variable.

A rule of thumb: If we need to use the `std::string` type, include the `<string>` header explicitly.

A Pointer to a String

A string has a member function `.c_str()` which returns a pointer to its first element. It is also said it returns a pointer to a null-terminated character array our string is made of:

```
#include <iostream>
#include <string>

int main()
{
    std::string s = "Hello World.";
    std::cout << s.c_str();
}
```

   Output:

```
Hello World.
```

This member function is of type `const char*` and is useful when we want to pass our `std::string` variable to a function accepting a `const char*` parameter.

Substrings

We use the `.substr()` member function to create a substring from a string. The function returns a substring that starts at a certain position in the main string and is of a certain length. The signature of the function is *.substring(starting_position, length)*. Example:

```cpp
#include <iostream>
#include <string>

int main()
{
    std::string s = "Hello World.";
    std::string mysubstring = s.substr(6, 5);
    std::cout << "The substring value is: " << mysubstring;
}
```

Output:

```
The substring value is: World
```

In this example, we have the main string that holds the value of "Hello World." Then we create a substring that only has the "World" value. The substring starts from the sixth character of the main string, and its length is five characters.

Finding a Substring

To find a substring in a string, we use the `.find()` member function. It searches for the substring in a string. If the substring is found, the function returns the position of the first found substring. This position is the position of a character where the substring starts in the main string. If the substring is not found, the function returns a value that is *std::string::npos*. The function itself is of type *std::string::size_type*.

To find a substring "Hello" inside the "This is a Hello World string" string, we write

```cpp
#include <iostream>
#include <string>

int main()
{
    std::string s = "This is a Hello World string.";
    std::string stringtofind = "Hello";
    std::string::size_type found = s.find(stringtofind);
```

```
    if (found != std::string::npos)
    {
        std::cout << "Substring found at position: " << found;
    }
    else
    {
        std::cout << "The substring is not found.";
    }
}
```

Output:

```
Substring found at position: 10
```

Here, we have the main string and a substring we want to find. We supply the substring to the *.find()* function as an argument. We store the function's return value to a variable *found*. Then we check the value of this variable. If the value is not equal to *std::string::npos*, the substring is found. We print the message and the position of a character in the main string where our substring was found.

CHAPTER 14

Automatic Type Deduction

We can automatically deduce the type of an object using the auto specifier. The auto specifier deduces the type of an object based on the object's initializer type.

Example:

```
auto c = 'a';    // char type
```

This example deduces c to be of type char as the char literal 'a' is of type char. Similarly, we can have

```
auto x = 123;    // int type
```

Here, the compiler deduces the x to be of type int because an integer literal 123 is of type int.

The type can also be deduced based on the type of the expression:

```
auto d = 123.456 / 789.10;    // double
```

This example deduces d to be of type double as the type of the entire 123.456 / 789.10 expression is double.

We can use auto as part of the reference type:

```
int main()
{
    int x = 123;
    auto& y = x; // y is of int& type
}
```

© Slobodan Dmitrović 2023
S. Dmitrović, *Modern C++ for Absolute Beginners*, https://doi.org/10.1007/978-1-4842-9274-7_14

or as part of the constant type:

```
int main()
{
    const auto x = 123; // x is of const int type
}
```

We use the *auto* specifier when the type (name) is hard to deduce manually or cumbersome to type due to its length.

CHAPTER 15

Exercises

Array Definition

Write a program that defines and initializes an array of five doubles. Change and then print out the values of the first and last array elements.

```cpp
#include <iostream>

int main()
{
    double arr[5] = { 1.23, 2.45, 8.52, 6.3, 10.15 };
    arr[0] = 2.56;
    arr[4] = 3.14;
    std::cout << "The first array element is: " << arr[0] << '\n';
    std::cout << "The last array element is: " << arr[4] << '\n';
}
```

Output:

```
The first array element is: 2.56
The last array element is: 3.14
```

© Slobodan Dmitrović 2023
S. Dmitrović, *Modern C++ for Absolute Beginners*, https://doi.org/10.1007/978-1-4842-9274-7_15

Pointer to an Object

Write a program that defines an object of type double. Define a pointer that points to that object. Print the value of the pointed-to object by dereferencing a pointer.

```
#include <iostream>

int main()
{                                                    .
    double d = 3.14;
    double* p = &d;
    std::cout << "The value of the pointed-to object is: " << *p;
}
```

   Output:

```
The value of the pointed-to object is: 3.14
```

Reference Type

Write a program that defines an object of type double called mydouble. Define an object of reference type called myreference and initialize it with mydouble. Change the value of myreference. Print the object value using both the reference and the original variable. Change the value of mydouble. Print the value of both objects.

```
#include <iostream>

int main()
{
    double mydouble = 3.14;
    double& myreference = mydouble;
    myreference = 6.28;
    std::cout << "The values are: " << mydouble << " and " << myreference
    << '\n';
    mydouble = 9.45;
    std::cout << "The values are: " << mydouble << " and " << myreference
    << '\n';
}
```

Output:

```
The values are: 6.28 and 6.28
The values are: 9.45 and 9.45
```

Strings

Write a program that defines two strings. Join them together and assign the result to a third string. Print out the value of the resulting string.

```cpp
#include <iostream>
#include <string>

int main()
{
    std::string s1 = "Hello";
    std::string s2 = " World!";
    std::string s3 = s1 + s2;
    std::cout << "The resulting string is: " << s3;
}
```

Output:

```
The resulting string is: Hello World!
```

Strings from Standard Input

Write a program that accepts the first and the last name from the standard input using the std::getline function. Store the input in a single string called fullname. Print out the string.

```cpp
#include <iostream>
#include <string>

int main()
{
    std::string fullname;
    std::cout << "Please enter the first and the last name: ";
    std::getline(std::cin, fullname);
    std::cout << "Your name is: " << fullname;
}
```

Possible Output:

```
Please enter the first and the last name: John Doe
Your name is: John Doe
```

Creating a Substring

Write a program that creates two substrings from the main string. The main string is made up of first and last names and is equal to "John Doe." The first substring is the first name. The second substring is the last name. Print the main string and two substrings afterward.

```cpp
#include <iostream>
#include <iostream>

int main()
{
    std::string fullname = "John Doe";
    std::string firstname = fullname.substr(0, 4);
    std::string lastname = fullname.substr(5, 3);
    std::cout << "The full name is: " << fullname << '\n';
    std::cout << "The first name is: " << firstname << '\n';
    std::cout << "The last name is: " << lastname << '\n';
}
```

Output:

```
The full name is: John Doe
The first name is: John
The last name is: Doe
```

Finding a Single Character

Write a program that defines the main string with a value of "Hello C++ World." and checks if a single character 'C' is found in the main string.

```cpp
#include <iostream>
#include <string>

int main()
{
    std::string s = "Hello C++ World.";
    char c = 'C';
    auto characterfound = s.find(c);
    if (characterfound != std::string::npos)
    {
        std::cout << "Character found at position: " << characterfound
        << '\n';
    }
    else
    {
        std::cout << "Character was not found." << '\n';
    }
}
```

Output:

```
Character found at position: 6
```

Finding a Substring

Write a program that defines the main string with a value of "Hello C++ World." and checks if a substring "C++" is found in the main string.

```cpp
#include <iostream>
#include <string>

int main()
{
    std::string s = "Hello C++ World.";
    std::string mysubstring = "C++";
    auto mysubstringfound = s.find(mysubstring);
    if (mysubstringfound != std::string::npos)
    {
        std::cout << "Substring found at position: " << mysubstringfound
        << '\n';
    }
    else
    {
        std::cout << "Substring was not found." << '\n';
    }
}
```

Output:

```
Substring found at position: 6
```

Both the 'C' character and the "C++" substring start at the same position in our main string. That is why both examples yield a value of six.

Instead of typing the lengthy std::string::size_type type for our characterfound and mysubstringfound variables, we used the auto specifier to deduce the type for us automatically.

Automatic Type Deduction

Write a program that automatically deduces the type for char, int, and double objects based on the initializer used. Print out the values afterward.

```
#include <iostream>

int main()
{
    auto c = 'a';
    auto x = 123;
    auto d = 3.14;
    std::cout << "The type of c is deduced as char, the value is: "
    << c << '\n';
    std::cout << "The type of x is deduced as int, the value is: "
    << x << '\n';
    std::cout << "The type of d is deduced as double, the value is: "
    << d << '\n';
}
```

Output:

```
The type of c is deduced as char, the value is: a
The type of x is deduced as int, the value is: 123
The type of d is deduced as double, the value is: 3.14
```

CHAPTER 16

Statements

Earlier, we described statements as commands, pieces of code that are executed in some order. Expressions ending with a semicolon are statements. The C++ language also comes with some built-in statements. We will start with the *selection statements*.

Selection Statements

Selection statements allow us to execute the appropriate statements based on some given condition.

if Statement

When we want to execute a statement or more statements based on some condition, we use the if statement. The if statement has the format of

```
if (condition) statement(s)
```

The statement(s) part executes only if the condition is true. Example:

```
#include <iostream>

int main()
{
    bool b = true;
    if (b) std::cout << "The condition is true.";
}
```

Output:

```
The condition is true.
```

© Slobodan Dmitrović 2023
S. Dmitrović, *Modern C++ for Absolute Beginners*, https://doi.org/10.1007/978-1-4842-9274-7_16

To execute multiple statements if the condition is true, we use the block scope {}:

```cpp
#include <iostream>

int main()
{
    bool b = true;
    if (b)
    {
        std::cout << "This is the first statement.";
        std::cout << "\nThis is a second statement.";
    }
}
```

Output:

```
This is the first statement.
This is a second statement.
```

Another form is the if-else statement:

```cpp
if (condition) statement(s) else other_statement(s)
```

If the condition is true, the first statement(s) executes. Otherwise, the second other_statement(s) after the else keyword executes. Example:

```cpp
#include <iostream>

int main()
{
    bool b = false;
    if (b) std::cout << "The condition is true.";
    else std::cout << "The condition is false.";
}
```

Output:

```
The condition is false.
```

To execute multiple statements in either `if` or `else` branch, we use brace-enclosed blocks {}:

```cpp
#include <iostream>

int main()
{
    bool b = false;
    if (b)
    {
        std::cout << "The condition is true.";
        std::cout << "\nThis is the second statement.";
    }
    else
    {
        std::cout << "The condition is false.";
        std::cout << "\nThis is the second statement.";
    }
}
```

Output:

```
The condition is false.
This is the second statement.
```

Conditional Expression

An expression that returns a value based on a condition is called a *conditional expression*. First, let us have a simple if statement example:

```cpp
#include <iostream>

int main()
{
    bool mycondition = true;
    int x = 0;
    if (mycondition)
    {
```

```
        x = 1;
    }
    else
    {
        x = 0;
    }
    std::cout << "The value of x is: " << x << '\n';
}
```

Output:

```
The value of x is: 1
```

To rewrite the previous example using a *conditional expression,* we write

```
#include <iostream>

int main()
{
    bool mycondition = true;
    int x = 0;
    x = (mycondition) ? 1 : 0;
    std::cout << "The value of x is: " << x << '\n';
}
```

Output:

```
The value of x is: 1
```

The conditional expression is of the following syntax:

```
(condition) ? expression_1 : expression_2
```

The *conditional expression* uses the unary ? operator, which checks the value of the condition. If the condition is true, it returns *expression_1*. If the condition is false, it returns *expression_2*. It can be thought of as a way of replacing a simple if-else statement with a one-liner.

The Logical Operators

The logical operators perform logical *and*, *or*, and *negation* operations on their operands. The first is the && operator, which is a logical AND operator. The result of a logical AND condition with two operands is true if both operands are true. Example:

```cpp
#include <iostream>

int main()
{
    bool a = true;
    bool b = true;
    if (a && b)
    {
        std::cout << "The entire condition is true.";
    }
    else
    {
        std::cout << "The entire condition is false.";
    }
}
```

Output:

```
The entire condition is true.
```

The next operator is ||, which is a logical OR operator. The result of a logical OR expression is always true except when both operands are false. Example:

```cpp
#include <iostream>

int main()
{
    bool a = false;
    bool b = false;
    if (a || b)
    {
        std::cout << "The entire condition is true.";
    }
```

```
    else
    {
        std::cout << "The entire condition is false.";
    }
}
```

Output:

```
The entire condition is false.
```

The next logical operator is the negation operator, represented by a ! symbol. It negates the value of its only right-hand-side operand. It turns the value of true to false and vice versa. Example:

```
#include <iostream>

int main()
{
    bool a = true;
    if (!a)
    {
        std::cout << "The condition is true.";
    }
    else
    {
        std::cout << "The condition is false.";
    }
}
```

Output:

```
The condition is false.
```

Comparison Operators

Comparison operators allow us to compare the values of operands. Comparison operators are less than <, less than or equal to <=, greater than >, greater than or equal to >=, equal to ==, and not equal to ! =.

We can use the equality operator == to check if the values of operands are equal:

```cpp
#include <iostream>

int main()
{
    int x = 5;
    if (x == 5)
    {
        std::cout << "The value of x is equal to 5.";
    }
}
```

Output:

```
The value of x is equal to 5.
```

Here's the use case for other comparison operators:

```cpp
#include <iostream>

int main()
{
    int x = 10;
    if (x > 5)
    {
        std::cout << "The value of x is greater than 5.";
    }
    if (x >= 10)
    {
        std::cout << "\nThe value of x is greater than or equal to 10.";
    }
```

```
    if (x != 20)
    {
        std::cout << "\nThe value of x is not equal to 20.";
    }
    if (x == 20)
    {
        std::cout << "\nThe value of x is equal to 20.";
    }
}
```

Output:

```
The value of x is greater than 5.
The value of x is greater than or equal to 10.
The value of x is not equal to 20.
```

Now, we can use both logical and comparison operators in the same condition:

```
#include <iostream>

int main()
{
    int x = 10;
    if (x > 5 && x < 15)
    {
        std::cout << "The value of x is greater than 5 and less than 15.";
    }
    bool b = true;
    if (x >5 && b)
    {
        std::cout << "\nThe value of x is greater than 5 and b is true.";
    }
}
```

Output:

```
The value of x is greater than 5 and less than 15.
The value of x is greater than 5 and b is true.
```

Any literal, object or expression, implicitly convertible to true or false, can be used as a condition:

```cpp
#include <iostream>

int main()
{
    if (1) // literal 1 is convertible to true
    {
        std::cout << "The condition is true.";
    }
}
```

Output:

```
The condition is true.
```

If we used an integer variable with a value other than 0, the result would be true:

```cpp
#include <iostream>

int main()
{
    int x = 10; // if x was 0, the condition would be false
    if (x)
    {
        std::cout << "The condition is true.";
    }
    else
    {
        std::cout << "The condition is false.";
    }
}
```

Output:

```
The condition is true.
```

It is good practice to use the code blocks {} inside the `if` statement branches, even if there is only one statement to be executed.

switch Statement

The switch statement is similar to having multiple if statements. It checks the value of the condition (which must be an integral or enum value) and, based on that value, executes the code inside one of a given set of `case:` labels. If none of the case statements is equal to the condition, the code inside the `default:` label is executed. General syntax:

```
switch (condition)
{
case value1:
    statement(s);
    break;
case value2etc:
    statement(s);
    break;
default:
    statement(s);
    break;
}
```

Here's a simple example that checks for the value of integer x and executes the appropriate case label:

```
#include <iostream>

int main()
{
    int x = 3;
    switch (x)
    {
```

```
case 1:
    std::cout << "The value of x is 1.";
    break;
case 2:
    std::cout << "The value of x is 2.";
    break;
case 3:
    std::cout << "The value of x is 3."; // this statement will be
    // executed
    break;
default:
    std::cout << "The value is none of the above.";
    break;
}
}
```

Output:

```
The value of x is 3.
```

The break statement exits the entire switch statement. If there were no break statements, the code would *fall through* to the next case statement and execute the code there regardless of the x value. We need to put breaks in all the case: and default: switches.

Iteration Statements

If we need some code to execute multiple times, we use *iteration statements*. Iteration statements are statements that execute some code in a loop. The code in the loop executes zero, one, or multiple times, depending on the statement and the condition.

for Statement

The for statement executes code in a loop. The execution depends on the condition. The general syntax of the for statement is

```
for (init_statement; condition; iteration_expression)
{ statement(s) }
```

Here is a simple example that executes a code ten times:

```cpp
#include <iostream>

int main()
{
    for (int i = 0; i < 10; i++)
    {
        std::cout << "The counter is: " << i << '\n';
    }
}
```

Output:

```
The counter is: 0
The counter is: 1
The counter is: 2
The counter is: 3
The counter is: 4
The counter is: 5
The counter is: 6
The counter is: 7
The counter is: 8
The counter is: 9
```

This example executes the code inside the for loop ten times. The init_statement is int i = 0;. We initialize the counter to 0. The condition is i < 10; and the iteration_ expression is i++;.

A simple explanation:

Initialize a counter to 0, check if the counter is less than 10, execute the std::cout << "The counter is: " << i << '\n'; statement inside the code block, and increment the counter i by 1. So, the code inside the code block will continue executing as long as the i < 10 condition is true. Once the counter becomes 10, the condition is no longer true, and the for loop terminates.

If we wanted something to execute, let us say, five times, we would set a different condition:

```
#include <iostream>

int main()
{
    for (int i = 0; i < 5; i++)
    {
        std::cout << "The counter is: " << i << '\n';
    }
}
```

Output:

```
The counter is: 0
The counter is: 1
The counter is: 2
The counter is: 3
The counter is: 4
```

while Statement

The while statement executes code as long as the condition is true. The syntax for the while loop is

```
while (condition) { // execute some code }
```

As long as the condition is `true`, the `while` loop will continue executing the code. When the `condition` becomes `false`, the `while` loop terminates. Example:

```
#include <iostream>

int main()
{
    int x = 0;
    while (x < 10)
    {
        std::cout << "The value of x is: " << x << '\n';
        x++;
    }
}
```

Output:

```
The value of x is: 0
The value of x is: 1
The value of x is: 2
The value of x is: 3
The value of x is: 4
The value of x is: 5
The value of x is: 6
The value of x is: 7
The value of x is: 8
The value of x is: 9
```

The code in this example executes ten times. After each iteration, the condition x < 10 is evaluated, and as long as it is equal to `true`, the code in the code block will keep executing. Once the condition becomes `false`, the `while` loop terminates. In this example, we increment the value of x in each iteration. And once it becomes 10, the loop terminates.

do Statement

The do statement is similar to the while statement, but the condition comes after the body. The code inside the do statement is guaranteed to execute at least once. The syntax is

```
do { // execute some code } while (condition);
```

If we used the previous example, the code would be

```cpp
#include <iostream>

int main()
{
    int x = 0;
    do
    {
        std::cout << "The value of x is: " << x << '\n';
        x++;
    } while (x < 10);
}
```

Output:

```
The value of x is: 0
The value of x is: 1
The value of x is: 2
The value of x is: 3
The value of x is: 4
The value of x is: 5
The value of x is: 6
The value of x is: 7
The value of x is: 8
The value of x is: 9
```

The do statement is rarely used and better avoided.

Please note that there is also an iteration statement called *the range-for statement*. We will talk about it when we explain the containers later on.

CHAPTER 17

Constants

When we want to have a read-only object or promise not to change the value of some object in the current scope, we make it a constant. C++ uses the const type qualifier to mark the object as a read-only. We say that our object is now *immutable*. To define an integer constant with a value of five, for example, we would write

```
int main()
{
    const int n = 5;
}
```

We can now use that constant in places such as an array size:

```
int main()
{
    const int n = 5;
    int arr[n] = { 10, 20, 30, 40, 50 };
}
```

Constants are not modifiable. Attempting to modify their values results in a compile-time error:

```
int main()
{
    const int n = 5;
    n++; // error, can't modify a read-only object
}
```

© Slobodan Dmitrović 2023
S. Dmitrović, *Modern C++ for Absolute Beginners*, https://doi.org/10.1007/978-1-4842-9274-7_17

An object declared const cannot be assigned to, it can only be initialized. So, we can't have:

```
int main()
{
    const int n;        // error, no initializer
    const int m = 123; // OK
}
```

Worth noticing is that const modifies an entire type, not just the object. So, const int and int are two different types. The first one is said to be const qualified.

Another const qualifier is the constant expression named constexpr. It is a constant that can be evaluated at compile time. Initializers for constant expressions can be evaluated at compile time and must themselves be constant expressions. Example:

```
int main()
{
    constexpr int n = 123;          //OK, 123 is a compile-time constant
                                    // expression
    constexpr double d = 456.78;    //OK, 456.78 is a compile-time constant
                                    // expression
    constexpr double d2 = d;        //OK, d is a constant expression
    int x = 123;
    constexpr int n2 = x;           //compile-time error
                                    // the value of x is not known during
                                    // compile-time

}
```

CHAPTER 18

Exercises

A Simple if Statement

Write a program that defines a boolean variable whose value is false. Use the variable as the condition inside the if statement.

```cpp
#include <iostream>

int main()
{
    bool mycondition = false;
    if (mycondition)
    {
        std::cout << "The condition is true." << '\n';
    }
    else
    {
        std::cout << "The condition is not true." << '\n';
    }
}
```

Output:

```
The condition is not true.
```

© Slobodan Dmitrović 2023
S. Dmitrović, *Modern C++ for Absolute Beginners*, https://doi.org/10.1007/978-1-4842-9274-7_18

Logical Operators

Write a program that defines a variable of type int. Assign the value of 256 to the variable. Check if the value of this variable is greater than 100 and less than 300. Then, define a boolean variable with a value of true. Check if the int number is greater than 100 or if the value of a bool variable is true. Then define a second bool variable whose value will be the negation of the first bool variable.

```
#include <iostream>

int main()
{
    int x = 256;
    if (x > 100 && x < 300)
    {
        std::cout << "The value is greater than 100 and less than 300.
        " << '\n';
    }
    else
    {
        std::cout << "The value is not inside the (100 .. 300) range.
        " << '\n';
    }
    bool mycondition = true;
    if (x > 100 || mycondition)
    {
        std::cout << "Either x is greater than 100 or the bool variable is
        true." << '\n';
    }
    else
    {
        std::cout << "x is not greater than 100 and the bool variable is
        false." << '\n';
    }
    bool mysecondcondition = !mycondition;
}
```

Output:

The value is greater than 100 and less than 300.
Either x is greater than 100 or the bool variable is true.

The switch Statement

Write a program that defines a simple integer variable with a value of three. Use the switch statement to check if the value is inside the [1..4] range.

```
#include <iostream>

int main()
{
    int x = 3;
    switch (x)
    {
    case 1:
        std::cout << "The value is equal to 1." << '\n';
        break;
    case 2:
        std::cout << "The value is equal to 2." << '\n';
        break;
    case 3:
        std::cout << "The value is equal to 3." << '\n';
        break;
    case 4:
        std::cout << "The value is equal to 4." << '\n';
        break;
    default:
        std::cout << "The value is not inside the [1..4] range." << '\n';
        break;
    }
}
```

Output:

```
The value is equal to 3.
```

The for Loop

Write a program that uses a for loop to print out the counter's value ten times. The counter starts at zero.

```cpp
#include <iostream>

int main()
{
    for (int i = 0; i < 10; i++)
    {
        std::cout << "The counter is now: " << i << '\n';
    }
}
```

Output:

```
The counter is now: 0
The counter is now: 1
The counter is now: 2
The counter is now: 3
The counter is now: 4
The counter is now: 5
The counter is now: 6
The counter is now: 7
The counter is now: 8
The counter is now: 9
```

Array and the for Loop

Write a program that defines an array of five integers. Use the for loop to print the array elements and their indexes.

```cpp
#include <iostream>

int main()
{
    int arr[5] = { 3, 20, 8, 15, 10 };
    for (int i = 0; i < 5; i++)
    {
        std::cout << "arr[" << i << "] = " << arr[i] << '\n';
    }
}
```

Output:

```
arr[0] = 3
arr[1] = 20
arr[2] = 8
arr[3] = 15
arr[4] = 10
```

Explanation: Here, we defined an array of five elements. Arrays are indexed starting from zero. So the first array element 3 has an index of 0. The last array element of 10 has an index of 4. We used the for loop to iterate over array elements and print both their indexes and values. Our for loop starts with a counter of 0 and ends with a counter of 4.

The const Type Qualifier

Write a program that defines three objects of type const int, const double, and const std::string, respectively. Define a fourth const int object and initialize it with a value of the first const int object. Print out the values of all the variables.

```cpp
#include <iostream>

int main()
{
    const int c1 = 123;
    const double d = 456.789;
    const std::string s = "Hello World!";
    const int c2 = c1;
    std::cout << "Constant integer c1 value: " << c1 << '\n';
    std::cout << "Constant double d value: " << d << '\n';
    std::cout << "Constant std::string s value: " << s << '\n';
    std::cout << "Constant integer c2 value: " << c2 << '\n';
}
```

Output:

```
Constant integer c1 value: 123
Constant double d value: 456.789
Constant std::string s value: Hello World!
Constant integer c2 value: 123
```

CHAPTER 19

Functions

Introduction

We can break our C++ code into smaller chunks called functions. A function has a return type, a name, a list of parameters in a declaration, and an additional function body in a definition. A simple function definition is:

```
type function_name(arguments) {
    statement(s);
    return something;
}
```

Function Declaration

To declare a function, we need to specify a return type, a name, and a list of parameters, if any. To declare a function called myfunction of type void that accepts no parameters, we write:

```
void myvoidfunction();

int main()
{
}
```

Type void is a type that represents *nothing*, an empty set of values. To declare a function of type int accepting one parameter, we can write:

```
int mysquarednumber (int x);
```

© Slobodan Dmitrović 2023
S. Dmitrović, *Modern C++ for Absolute Beginners*, https://doi.org/10.1007/978-1-4842-9274-7_19

```
int main()
{
}
```

To declare a function of type `int`, which accepts, for example, two `int` parameters, we can write:

```
int mysum(int x, int y);

int main()
{
}
```

In function declaration only, we can also omit the parameter names, but we need to specify their types:

```
int mysum(int, int);

int main()
{
}
```

Function Definition

To be called in a program, a function must be defined first. A function definition has everything a function declaration has, plus the body of a function. Those are a return type, a function name, a list of function parameters, if any, and a function body. Example:

```
#include <iostream>

void myfunction(); // function declaration

int main()
{
}
```

```
// function definition
void myfunction() {
    std::cout << "Hello World from a function.";
}
```

To define a function that accepts one parameter, we can write:

```
int mysquarednumber(int x); // function declaration

int main()
{
}

// function definition
int mysquarednumber(int x) {
    return x * x;
}
```

To define a function that accepts two parameters, we can write:

```
int mysum(int x, int y); // function declaration

int main()
{
}

// function definition
int mysum(int x, int y) {
    return x + y;
}
```

To call the preceding function in our program, we specify the function name followed by empty parentheses ( ) (a function call operator) as the function has no parameters:

```
#include <iostream>

void myfunction(); // function declaration

int main()
```

```
{
    myfunction(); // a call to a function
}

// function definition
void myfunction() {
    std::cout << "Hello World from a function.";
}
```

Output:

```
Hello World from a function.
```

To call a function that accepts one parameter, we can use:

```
#include <iostream>

int mysquarednumber(int x); // function declaration

int main()
{
    int myresult = mysquarednumber(2); // a call to the function
    std::cout << "Number 2 squared is: " << myresult;
}

// function definition
int mysquarednumber(int x) {
    return x * x;
}
```

Output:

```
Number 2 squared is: 4
```

We called a function mysquarednumber by its name and supplied a value of 2 in place of the function parameter and assigned the result of a function to our myresult variable. What we pass into a function is often referred to as a *function argument*.

To call a function that accepts two or more arguments, we use the function name followed by an opening parenthesis, followed by a list of arguments separated by commas, and, finally, closing parentheses. Example:

```cpp
#include <iostream>

int mysum(int x, int y);

int main()
{
    int myresult = mysum(5, 10);
    std::cout << "The sum of 5 and 10 is: " << myresult;
}

int mysum(int x, int y) {
    return x + y;
}
```

Output:

```
The sum of 5 and 10 is: 15
```

Return Statement

Functions are of a certain type, also referred to as a *return type*, and they must return a value. The value returned is specified by a return statement. Functions of type void do not need a return statement. Example:

```cpp
#include <iostream>

void voidfn();

int main()
{
    voidfn();
}
```

```
void voidfn()
{
    std::cout << "This is a void function and needs no return.";
}
```

Output:

```
This is a void function and needs no return.
```

Functions of other, nonvoid types (except function main) need a `return` statement:

```
#include <iostream>

int intfn();

int main()
{
    std::cout << "The function returned a value of: " << intfn();
}

int intfn()
{
    return 42; // return statement
}
```

Output:

```
The function returned a value of: 42
```

A function can have multiple `return` statements if needed, but only one of those statements will be executed. Once any of the `return` statement is executed, the function exits and returns the control flow to the caller, and the rest of the code in the function is ignored:

```
#include <iostream>

int multiplereturns(int x);

int main()
{
```

```
    std::cout << "The value of a function is: " << multiplereturns(25);
}
int multiplereturns(int x)
{
    if (x >= 42)
    {
        return x;
    }
    return 0;
}
```

Output:

```
The value of a function is: 0
```

In short, the `return` statement does two things:

- Returns the control flow to a caller (in our examples, the caller was the function main())

- Returns the value (if any)

Passing Arguments

There are different ways of passing arguments to a function. Here, we will describe the three most used.

Passing by Value/Copy

When we pass an argument to a function, a copy of that argument is made and passed to the function if the function parameter type is not a reference. This means the value of the *original argument* does not change. An internal copy of the argument is made, and the function works with that copy. Example:

```
#include <iostream>

void myfunction(int byvalue)
{
```

```
    std::cout << "An argument passed by value: " << byvalue;
}

int main()
{
    myfunction(123);
}
```

   Output:

```
An argument passed by value: 123
```

This is known as passing an argument *by value* or passing an argument *by copy*.

Passing by Reference

When a function parameter type is a reference type, then the actual argument is passed to the function, not a copy of that argument. The function can now modify the value of the argument. Example:

```
#include <iostream>

void myfunction(int& byreference)
{
    byreference++; // we can modify the value of the argument
    std::cout << "An argument passed by reference: " << byreference;
}

int main()
{
    int x = 123;
    myfunction(x);
}
```

   Output:

```
An argument passed by reference: 124
```

Here, we passed an argument of a reference type int&, so the function now works with the actual argument and can change its value. When passing by reference, we need to pass the variable itself; we can't pass in a literal representing a value. Passing by reference is best avoided.

Passing by Const Reference

What is preferred (for arguments of complex types) is passing an argument by *const reference*, also referred to as a *reference to const*. It can be more efficient to pass an argument by reference, but to ensure it is not changed, we make it of const reference type. Example:

```
#include <iostream>
#include <string>

void myfunction(const std::string& byconstreference)
{
    std::cout << "An argument passed by const reference: "
    << byconstreference;
}

int main()
{
    std::string s = "Hello World!";
    myfunction(s);
}
```

Output:

```
An argument passed by const reference: Hello World!
```

We use passing by const reference for efficiency reasons, and the const modifier ensures the value of an argument will not be changed.

In the last three examples, we omitted the function declarations and only supplied the function definitions. Although a function definition is also a declaration, you should provide both the declaration and a definition as in:

```
#include <iostream>
#include <string>

void myfunction(const std::string& byconstreference);

int main()
{
    std::string s = "Hello World!";
    myfunction(s);
}
void myfunction(const std::string& byconstreference)
{
    std::cout << "Arguments passed by const reference: "
    << byconstreference;
}
```

   Output:

```
Arguments passed by const reference: Hello World!
```

Function Overloading

We can have multiple functions with the same name but with different parameter types. This is called *function overloading*. A simple explanation: When the function names are the same, but the parameter types differ, then we have overloaded functions. Here's an example of function overload declarations:

```
void myprint(char param);
void myprint(int param);
void myprint(double param);
```

   Then we implement function definitions and call each one:

```
#include <iostream>

void myprint(char param);
void myprint(int param);
void myprint(double param);
```

```cpp
int main()
{
    myprint('c');          // calling char overload
    myprint(123);          // calling integer overload
    myprint(456.789);      // calling double overload
}

void myprint(char param)
{
    std::cout << "Printing a character: " << param << '\n';
}

void myprint(int param)
{
    std::cout << "Printing an integer: " << param << '\n';
}

void myprint(double param)
{
    std::cout << "Printing a double: " << param << '\n';
}
```

Output:

```
Printing a character: c
Printing an integer: 123
Printing a double: 456.789
```

When calling our functions, a proper overload is selected based on the type of argument we supply. In the first call to myprint('c'), a char overload is selected because the literal 'c' is of type char. In a second function call myprint(123), an integer overload is selected because the type of argument 123 is int. And lastly, in our last function call myprint(456.789), a double overload is selected by a compiler as the argument 456.789 is of type double.

Indeed, literals in C++ are also of certain types, and the C++ standard precisely defines what that type is. Here are some of the literals and their corresponding types:

```
'c'        -    char
123        -    int
123u       -    unsigned int
123ul      -    unsigned long
456.789    -    double
456.789f   -    float
true       -    boolean
"Hello"    -    const char[6]
```

CHAPTER 20

Exercises

Function Definition

Write a program that defines a function of type void called printmessage(). The function outputs a "Hello World from a function." message on the standard output. Call the function from main.

```cpp
#include <iostream>

void printmessage()
{
    std::cout << "Hello World from a function.";
}

int main()
{
    printmessage();
}
```

Output:

```
Hello World from a function.
```

Separate Declaration and Definition

Write a program that declares and defines a function of type void called printmessage(). The function outputs a "Hello World from a function." message on the standard output. Call the function from main.

© Slobodan Dmitrović 2023
S. Dmitrović, *Modern C++ for Absolute Beginners*, https://doi.org/10.1007/978-1-4842-9274-7_20

```
#include <iostream>

void printmessage(); // function declaration

int main()
{
    printmessage();
}

// function definition
void printmessage()
{
    std::cout << "Hello World from a function.";
}
```

Output:

```
Hello World from a function.
```

Function Parameters

Write a program that has a function of type int called multiplication accepting two int parameters by value. The function multiplies those two parameters and returns a result to itself. Invoke the function in the main() function, and assign a result of the function to a local int variable. Print the result in the console.

```
#include <iostream>

int multiplication(int x, int y)
{
    return x * y;
}

int main()
{
    int myresult = multiplication(10, 20);
    std::cout << "The result is: " << myresult;
}
```

Output:

```
The result is: 200
```

Passing Arguments

Write a program that has a function of type void called custommessage. The function accepts one parameter by reference to const of type std::string and outputs a custom message on the standard output using that parameter's value. Invoke the function in the main program with a local string.

```
#include <iostream>
#include <string>

void custommessage(const std::string& message)
{
    std::cout << "The string argument used is: " << message;
}

int main()
{
    std::string mymessage = "My Custom Message.";
    custommessage(mymessage);
}
```

Output:

```
The string argument used is: My Custom Message.
```

Function Overloads

Write a program that has two function overloads. The functions are called division, and both accept two parameters. They divide the parameters and return the result to themselves. The first function overload is of type int and has two parameters of type int. The second overload is of type double and accepts two parameters of type double. Invoke the appropriate overload in main, first by supplying integer arguments and then the double arguments. Observe different results.

```cpp
#include <iostream>
#include <string>

int division(int x, int y)
{
    return x / y;
}

double division(double x, double y)
{
    return x / y;
}

int main()
{
    std::cout << "Integer division: " << division(9, 2) << '\n';
    std::cout << "Floating point division: " << division(9.0, 2.0);
}
```

Output:

```
Integer division: 4
Floating point division: 4.5
```

CHAPTER 21

Scope and Lifetime

When we declare a variable, its name is valid only inside some sections of the source code. And that section (part, portion, region) of the source code is called *scope*. It is the region of code in which the name can be accessed. There are different scopes.

Local Scope

When we declare a name inside a function, that name has a *local scope*. Its scope starts from the point of declaration till the end of the function block marked with }.

Example:

```
void myfunction()
{
    int x = 123; // Here begins the x's scope
} // and here it ends
```

Our variable x is declared inside a myfunction() body, and it has a local scope. We say that name x is local to myfunction(). It exists (can be accessed) only inside the function's scope and nowhere else.

Block Scope

The block scope is a section of code marked by a block of code starting with { and ending with }. Example:

```
int main()
{
    int x = 123; // first x' scope begins here
    {
```

© Slobodan Dmitrović 2023
S. Dmitrović, *Modern C++ for Absolute Beginners*, https://doi.org/10.1007/978-1-4842-9274-7_21

```
    int x = 456; // redefinition of x, second x' scope begins here
} // block ends, second x' scope ends here
    // the first x resumes here
} // block ends, scope of first x's ends here
```

There are other scopes as well, which we will cover later in the book. It is important to introduce the notion of scope at this point to explain the object's lifetime.

Lifetime

The lifetime of an object is the time an object spends in memory. The lifetime is determined by a so-called *storage duration*. There are different kinds of storage durations.

Automatic Storage Duration

The automatic storage duration is a duration where memory for an object is automatically allocated at the beginning of a block and deallocated when the code block ends. This is also called *stack memory*; objects are allocated on the *stack*. In this case, the object's lifetime is determined by its scope. All local objects have this storage duration.

Dynamic Storage Duration

The dynamic storage duration is a duration where memory for an object is manually allocated and manually deallocated. This kind of storage is often referred to as *heap memory*. The user determines when the memory for an object will be allocated and when it will be released. The lifetime of an object is not determined by the scope in which the object was defined. We do it through operator *new* and *smart pointers*. In modern C++, we should prefer the smart pointer facilities to operator new.

Static Storage Duration

When an object declaration is prepended with a `static` specifier, it means the storage for a static object is allocated when the program starts and deallocated when the program ends. There is only one instance of such objects, and (with a few exceptions) their lifetime ends when a program ends. They are objects we can access at any given time during the execution of a program. We will talk about the static specifier and static initialization later in the book.

Operators new and delete

We can dynamically allocate and deallocate storage for our object and have pointers point to this newly allocated memory.

The operator `new` allocates space for an object. The object is allocated on the *free store*, often called *heap* or *heap memory*. The allocated memory must be deallocated using the operator `delete`. It deallocates the memory previously allocated with an operator `new`. Example:

```
#include <iostream>

int main()
{
    int* p = new int;
    *p = 123;
    std::cout << "The pointed-to value is: " << *p;
    delete p;
}
```

Output:

```
The pointed-to value is: 123
```

This example allocates space for one integer on the free store. Pointer p now points to the newly allocated memory for our integer. We can now assign a value to our newly allocated integer object by dereferencing a pointer. Finally, we free the memory by calling the operator `delete`.

If we want to allocate memory for an array, we use the operator new[ ]. To deallocate a memory allocated for an array, we use the operator delete[ ]. Pointers and arrays are similar and can often be used interchangeably. Pointers can be dereferenced by a subscript operator [ ]. Example:

```
#include <iostream>

int main()
{
    int* p = new int[3];
    p[0] = 1;
    p[1] = 2;
    p[2] = 3;
    std::cout << "The values are: " << p[0] << ' ' << p[1] << ' ' << p[2];
    delete[] p;
}
```

   Output:

```
The values are: 1 2 3
```

This example allocates space for three integers, an array of three integers, using the operator new[ ]. Our pointer p now points at the first element in the array. Then, using a subscript operator [ ], we dereference and assign a value to each array element. Finally, we deallocate the memory using the operator delete[ ]. Remember, always delete what you new-ed and always delete[ ] what you new[ ]-ed.

Remember: Prefer *smart pointers* to operator new. The lifetime of objects allocated on the free store is not bound by the scope in which the objects were defined. We manually allocate and manually deallocate the memory for our object, thus controlling when the object gets created and when it gets destroyed.

CHAPTER 22

Exercises

Automatic Storage Duration

Write a program that defines two variables of type int with automatic storage duration (placed on the stack) inside the main function scope.

```
#include <iostream>

int main()
{
    int x = 123;
    int y = 456;
    std::cout << "The values with automatic storage durations are: " << x
    << " and " << y;
}
```

Output:

```
The values with automatic storage durations are: 123 and 456
```

We can use the following image to visualize the placement of automatic storage objects called x and y:

© Slobodan Dmitrović 2023
S. Dmitrović, *Modern C++ for Absolute Beginners*, https://doi.org/10.1007/978-1-4842-9274-7_22

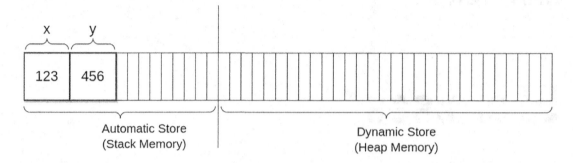

The memory for x and y will be automatically released when x and y go out of scope, which, in our case, is when they go out of the function main's scope (when the program ends). We do not need to release the memory for local (automatic) variables manually. We just let them *go out of scope*.

Dynamic Storage Duration

Write a program that defines a variable of type int*, which points to an object with dynamic storage duration (placed on the heap):

```
#include <iostream>

int main()
{
    int* p = new int{ 123 };
    std::cout << "The value with a dynamic storage duration is: " << *p;
    delete p;
}
```

Output:

```
The value with a dynamic storage duration is: 123
```

Explanation:

In this example, the object p only points at the object with dynamic storage duration (placed on heap memory) having the value of 123. The p object itself has an automatic storage duration and is placed on a stack. After a call to the int* p = new int{ 123 }; statement, our memory looks like the following:

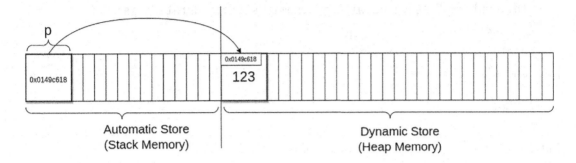

To delete the object on the heap, we need to use the *delete* operator. After a call to the delete p; statement, the pointed-to memory is released, and the diagram looks like the following:

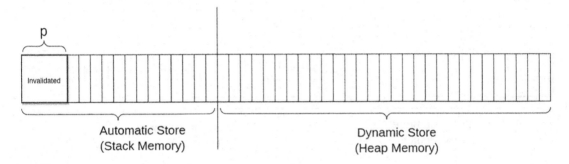

Automatic and Dynamic Storage Durations

Write a program that defines a variable of type int called x, having automatic storage duration, and a variable of type int*, which points to an object with dynamic storage duration. Both variables are in the same scope:

```cpp
#include <iostream>

int main()
{
    int x = 123; // automatic storage duration
    std::cout << "The value with an automatic storage duration is: " << x
    << '\n';
    int* p = new int{ x }; // allocate memory and copy the value
    from x to it
```

```
    std::cout << "The value with a dynamic storage duration is: "
    << *p << '\n';
    delete p;
} // end of scope here
```

Output:

```
The value with an automatic storage duration is: 123
The value with a dynamic storage duration is: 123
```

We can visualize the memory placement of objects using the following image:

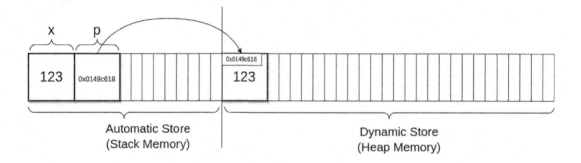

The local objects of type int called x, and the pointer p of type int*, reside in the automatic store memory (stack). The pointer is initialized with a dynamically allocated object on the heap memory that receives the copy of the value of x. Now both x and *p objects have the value of 123.

After the call to the delete p; statement, the dynamically allocated memory (object) is released, and now our diagram looks like the following:

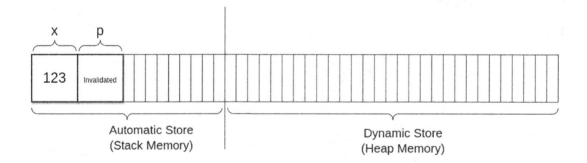

Classes – Introduction

A class is a user-defined type. It consists of members. The members are data members and member functions. A class can be described as data and some functionality on that data, wrapped into one. An instance of a class is called an object. To only declare a class name, we write

```
class MyClass;
```

To define an empty class, we add a class body marked by braces { }:

```
class MyClass{};
```

To create an instance of the class, an object, we use:

```
class MyClass{};

int main()
{
    MyClass o;
}
```

Explanation:
We defined a class called MyClass. Then we created an object o of type MyClass. It is said that o is an *object,* a *class instance.*

Data Member Fields

A class can have a set of some data in it. These are called *member fields.* Let us add one member field to our class and make it of type char:

© Slobodan Dmitrović 2023
S. Dmitrović, *Modern C++ for Absolute Beginners,* https://doi.org/10.1007/978-1-4842-9274-7_23

```
class MyClass
{
    char c;
};
```

Now our class has one data member field of type char called c. Let us now add two more fields of type int and double:

```
class MyClass
{
    char c;
    int x;
    double d;
};
```

Now our class has three member fields, and each member field has its name.

Member Functions

Similarly, a class can store functions. These are called *member functions*. They are mostly used to perform some operations on data fields. To declare a member function of type void called dosomething(), we write

```
class MyClass
{
    void dosomething();
};
```

There are two ways to define this member function. The first is to define it inside the class (body):

```
class MyClass
{
    void dosomething()
    {
        std::cout << "Hello World from a class.";
    }
};
```

The second one is to define it outside the class. In that case, we write the function type first, followed by a class name, followed by a scope resolution : : operator, followed by a function name, a list of parameters, if any, and a function body:

```
class MyClass
{
    void dosomething();
};

void MyClass::dosomething()
{
    std::cout << "Hello World from a class.";
}
```

Here, we declared a member function inside the class and defined it outside the class.

We can have multiple member functions in a class. To define them inside a class, we would write:

```
class MyClass
{
    void dosomething()
    {
        std::cout << "Hello World from a class.";
    }
    void dosomethingelse()
    {
        std::cout << "Hello Universe from a class.";
    }
};
```

To declare member functions inside a class and define them outside the class, we would write:

```
class MyClass
{
    void dosomething();
    void dosomethingelse();
};
```

```
void MyClass::dosomething()
{
    std::cout << "Hello World from a class.";
}

void MyClass::dosomethingelse()
{
    std::cout << "Hello Universe from a class.";
}
```

Now we can create a simple class that has both a data member field and a member function:

```
class MyClass
{
    int x;
    void printx()
    {
        std::cout << "The value of x is:" << x;
    }
};
```

This class has one data field of type int called x, and it has a member function called printx(). This member function reads the value of x and prints it out. This example is an introduction to member access specifiers or class member visibility.

Access Specifiers

Wouldn't it be convenient if there was a way we could disable access to member fields but allow access to member functions for our object and other entities accessing our class members? To place the code (of a class) into different levels of visibility? And that is what *access specifiers* are for. They specify access/visibility levels for class members. There are three access specifiers/labels – public, protected, and private:

```
class MyClass
{
public:
```

```
    // everything in here
    // has public access level
protected:
    // everything in here
    // has protected access level
private:
    // everything in here
    // has private access level
};
```

The default visibility/access specifier for a class is private if none of the access specifiers is present:

```
class MyClass
{
    // everything in here
    // has private access by default
};
```

Another way to write a class is to write a struct. A struct is also a class in which members have public access by default. So, a struct is the same thing as a class but with a public access specifier by default:

```
struct MyStruct
{
    // everything in here
    // is public by default
};
```

For now, we will focus only on public and private access specifiers. Public access members are accessible anywhere. For example, they are accessible to other class members and to objects of our class. To access a class member from an object, we use the dot . operator.

We said there are three different visibility levels (access specifiers) for a code inside a class. They are *private, protected,* and *public.* From whose perspective?

From the perspective of three different actors:

- A class itself
- A derived class
- An object of a class

A class itself can see and access any code inside a class, regardless of the visibility level.

A derived class can see and access only code inside a public and protected region.

An object of a class can see and access only code inside a public area.

Let's define a class where all the members have public access. To define a class with a public access specifier, we can write:

```
class MyClass
{
public:
    int x;
    void printx()
    {
        std::cout << "The value of x is:" << x;
    }
};
```

Let us instantiate this class and use it in our main program:

```
#include <iostream>

class MyClass
{
public:
    int x;
    void printx()
    {
        std::cout << "The value of data member x is: " << x;
    }
};
```

```
int main()
{
    MyClass o;
    o.x = 123;      // x is accessible to object o
    o.printx();     // printx() is accessible to object o
}
```

Output:

```
The value of data member x is: 123
```

Our object o now has direct access to all member fields as they are all marked public. Member fields always have access to each other regardless of the access specifier. That is why the member function printx() can access the member field x and print or change its value.

Private access members are accessible only to other class members (other code inside a class), not objects of a class. Example with full commentary:

```
#include <iostream>

class MyClass
{
private:
    int x; // x now has private access
public:
    void printx()
    {
        std::cout << "The value of x is:" << x; // x is accessible to
        // printx()
    }
};
```

```
int main()
{
    MyClass o;     // Create an object
    o.x = 123;     // Error, x has private access and is not accessible to
                   // object o
    o.printx();    // printx() is accessible from object o
}
```

Our object o now only has access to a member function `printx()` in the public section of the class. It cannot access members in the private section of the class.

If we want the class members to be accessible to our object, then we will put them inside the `public:` area. If we want the class members not to be accessible to our object, then we will put them in the `private:` section.

We want the data members to have private access and function members to have public access. This way, our object can access the member functions directly but not the member fields. There is another access specifier called `protected:` which we will talk about later in the book when we learn about inheritance.

Constructors

A constructor is a member function that has the same name as the class. The constructor's purpose is to initialize an object of a class. It constructs an object and can set values to data members. If a class has a constructor, all objects of that class will be initialized by a constructor call. In short, when an object is created, a code inside the constructor runs.

Default Constructor

A constructor without parameters or with default parameters set is called a *default constructor*. It is a constructor which can be called without arguments:

```
#include <iostream>

class MyClass
{
public:
    MyClass()
```

```
    {
        std::cout << "Default constructor invoked." << '\n';
    }
};
int main()
{
    MyClass o; // invoke a default constructor
}
```

Output:

```
Default constructor invoked.
```

Here's another example of a default constructor, the constructor with the default arguments set:

```
#include <iostream>

class MyClass
{
public:
    MyClass(int x = 123, int y = 456)
    {
        std::cout << "Default constructor invoked." << '\n';
    }
};

int main()
{
    MyClass o; // invoke a default constructor
}
```

Output:

```
Default constructor invoked.
```

If a default constructor is not explicitly defined in the code, the compiler will generate a default constructor. But when we define a constructor of our own, the one that needs parameters, the default constructor gets removed and is not generated by a compiler.

Constructors are invoked when object initialization takes place. They can't be invoked directly.

Constructors can have an arbitrary number of parameters, in which case we can call them *user-provided* constructors:

```cpp
#include <iostream>

class MyClass
{
public:
    int x, y;

    MyClass(int xx, int yy)
    {
        x = xx;
        y = yy;
    }
};

int main()
{
    MyClass o{ 1, 2 }; // invoke a user-provided constructor
    std::cout << "User-provided constructor invoked." << '\n';
    std::cout << o.x << ' ' << o.y;
}
```

Output:

```
User-provided constructor invoked.
1 2
```

In this example, our class has two data fields of type int and a constructor. The constructor accepts two parameters and assigns them to data members. We invoke the constructor by providing arguments in the initializer list with MyClass o{ 1, 2 };.

Constructors do not have a return type, they have the same name as the class, and their purpose is to initialize the object of their class.

Member Initialization

In our previous example, we used a constructor body and *assignments* to assign value to each class member. A better, more efficient way to initialize an object of a class is to use the constructor's *member initializer list* in the definition of the constructor:

```cpp
#include <iostream>

class MyClass
{
public:
    int x, y;
    MyClass(int xx, int yy)
        : x{ xx }, y{ yy } // member initializer list
    {
    }
};

int main()
{
    MyClass o{ 1, 2 }; // invoke a user-defined constructor
    std::cout << o.x << ' ' << o.y;
}
```

Output:

---

1 2

A member initializer list starts with a colon, followed by member names and their initializers, where each initialization expression is separated by a comma. In our previous example, an initialization list is the : x{ xx }, y{ yy } part. This is the preferred way of initializing class data members.

Copy Constructor

When we initialize an object of the class with another object of the same class, we invoke a copy constructor. If we do not supply our copy constructor, the compiler generates a default copy constructor that performs the so-called shallow copy. Example:

```
class MyClass
{
private:
    int x, y;
public:
    MyClass(int xx, int yy) : x{ xx }, y{ yy }
    {
    }
};

int main()
{
    MyClass o1{ 1, 2 };
    MyClass o2 = o1; // default copy constructor invoked
}
```

In this example, we initialize the object o2 with the object o1 of the same type. This invokes the default copy constructor.

We can provide our own copy constructor. The copy constructor has a special parameter signature of MyClass(const MyClass& rhs). Here's an example of a user-defined copy constructor:

```
#include <iostream>

class MyClass
{
```

```
private:
    int x, y;
public:
    MyClass(int xx, int yy) : x{ xx }, y{ yy }
    {
    }
    // user defined copy constructor
    MyClass(const MyClass& rhs)
        : x{ rhs.x }, y{ rhs.y } // initialize members with other object's
        // members
    {
        std::cout << "User-defined copy constructor invoked.";
    }
};

int main()
{
    MyClass o1{ 1, 2 };
    MyClass o2 = o1; // user defined copy constructor invoked
}
```

Output:

```
User-defined copy constructor invoked.
```

Here, we defined our own copy constructor in which we explicitly initialized data members with other objects' data members, and we printed out a simple message on the console/standard output.

Please note that the default copy constructor does not *correctly* copy members of some types, such as pointers, arrays, etc. In order to make copies properly, we need to define our own copy logic inside the copy constructor. This is referred to as a *deep copy*. For pointers, for example, we need to both create a pointer and assign a value to the object it points to in our user-defined copy constructor:

```cpp
#include <iostream>

class MyClass
{
private:
    int x;
    int* p;
public:
    MyClass(int xx, int pp)
        : x{ xx }, p{ new int{pp} }
    {
    }
MyClass(const MyClass& rhs)
        : x{ rhs.x }, p{ new int {*rhs.p} }
    {
        std::cout << "User-defined copy constructor invoked.";
    }
};

int main()
{
    MyClass o1{ 1, 2 };
    MyClass o2 = o1; // user defined copy constructor invoked
}
```

Output:

```
User-defined copy constructor invoked.
```

Here, we have two constructors: one is a user-provided regular constructor, and the other is a user-defined copy constructor. The first constructor initializes an object and is invoked here: MyClass o1{ 1, 2 }; in our main function.

The second, user-defined copy constructor is invoked here: MyClass o2 = o1;. This constructor now properly copies the values from both int and int* member fields.

In this example, we have pointers as member fields. If we had left out the user-defined copy constructor and relied on a default copy constructor, only the int member field would be properly copied, and the pointer would not. In this example, we rectified that.

In addition to copying, there is also a *move semantic*, where data is moved from one object to the other. This semantic is represented through a *move constructor* and a *move assignment* operator.

Copy Assignment

So far, we have used copy constructors to initialize one object with another object. We can also copy the values to an object after it has been initialized/created. We use a *copy assignment* for that. Simply, when we initialize an object with another object using the = operator on the same line, then the copy operation uses the copy constructor:

```
MyClass copyfrom;
MyClass copyto = copyfrom; // on the same line, uses a copy constructor
```

When an object is created on one line and then assigned to in the next line, it then uses the *copy assignment* operator to copy the data from another object:

```
MyClass copyfrom;
MyClass copyto;
copyto = copyfrom; // uses a copy assignment operator
```

A copy assignment operator is of the following signature:

```
MyClass& operator=(const MyClass& rhs)
```

To define a user-defined copy assignment operator inside a class, we use

```
class MyClass
{
public:
    MyClass& operator=(const MyClass& rhs)
    {
        // implement the copy logic here
        return *this;
    }
};
```

Notice that the overloaded operators having the = symbol must return a dereferenced `this` pointer at the end. To define a user-defined copy assignment operator outside the class, we use

```
class MyClass
{
public:
    MyClass& operator=(const MyClass& rhs);
};
MyClass& MyClass::operator=(const MyClass& rhs)
{
    // implement the copy logic here
    return *this;
}
```

Similarly, there is a *move assignment* operator, which we will discuss later in the book. More on operator overloading in the following chapters.

Move Constructor

In addition to copying, we can also move the data from one object to the other. We call it a *move semantics*. Move semantics is achieved through a move constructor and move assignment operator. The object from which the data was moved is left in some valid but unspecified state. The move operation is efficient in terms of speed of execution, as we do not have to make copies.

Move constructor accepts something called *rvalue reference* as an argument.

Every expression can find itself on the left-hand side or the right-hand side of the assignment operator. The expressions that can be used on the left-hand side are called lvalues, such as variables, function calls, class members, etc. The expressions that can be used on the right-hand side of an assignment operator are called rvalues, such as literals and other expressions.

Now the move semantics accepts a reference to that rvalue. The signature of an rvalue reference type is *T&&*, with double reference symbols. So, the signature of a move constructor is

```
MyClass (MyClass&& rhs)
```

To cast something to an rvalue reference, we use the *std::move* function. This function casts the object to an rvalue reference. It does not move anything. Here's an example where a move constructor is invoked:

```
#include <iostream>

class MyClass { };

int main()
{
    MyClass o1;
    MyClass o2 = std::move(o1);
    std::cout << "Move constructor invoked.";
    // or MyClass o2{std::move(o1)};
}
```

Output:

```
Move constructor invoked.
```

In this example, we define an object of type MyClass called o1. Then we initialize the second object o2 by moving everything from object o1 to o2. To do that, we need to cast the o2 to an rvalue reference with std::move(o1). This, in turn, invokes the MyClass move constructor for o2.

If a user does not provide a move constructor, the compiler provides an implicitly generated default move constructor.

Let us specify our own user-defined move constructor:

```
#include <iostream>
#include <string>

class MyClass
{
private:
    int x;
    std::string s;
```

```
public:
    MyClass(int xx, std::string ss) // user-provided constructor
        : x{ xx }, s{ ss }
    {}
    MyClass(MyClass&& rhs) // move constructor
        :
        x{ std::move(rhs.x) }, s{ std::move(rhs.s) }
    {
        std::cout << "Move constructor invoked." << '\n';
    }
};

int main()
{
    MyClass o1{ 1, "Some string value" };
    MyClass o2 = std::move(o1);
}
```

Output:

```
Move constructor invoked.
```

This example defines a class with two data members and two constructors. The first constructor is user provided, and it is used to initialize data members using provided arguments.

The second constructor is a user-defined move constructor accepting an rvalue reference parameter of type MyClass&& called rhs. This parameter will become our std::move(o1) argument/object. Then in the constructor initializer list, we also use the std::move function to move the data fields from o1 to o2.

Move Assignment

The move assignment operator is invoked when we declare an object and then try to assign an rvalue reference to it. This is done via the *move assignment* operator. The signature of the move assignment operator is MyClass& operator=(MyClass&& otherobject).

CHAPTER 23   CLASSES – INTRODUCTION

To define a user-defined move assignment operator inside a class, we use

```
class MyClass
{
public:
    MyClass& operator=(MyClass&& otherobject)
    {
        // implement the copy logic here
        return *this;
    }
};
```

As with any assignment operator overloading, we must return a dereferenced this pointer at the end. To define a move assignment operator outside the class, we use

```
class MyClass
{
public:
    MyClass& operator=(MyClass&& rhs);
};
MyClass& MyClass::operator=(MyClass&& rhs)
{
    // implement the copy logic here
    return *this;
}
```

A move assignment operator example adapted from a move constructor example would be

```
#include <iostream>
#include <string>

class MyClass
{
private:
    int x;
    std::string s;
```

```cpp
public:
    MyClass(int xx, std::string ss) // user-provided constructor
        : x{ xx }, s{ ss }
    {}
    MyClass& operator=(MyClass&& otherobject) // move assignment operator
    {
        x = std::move(otherobject.x);
        s = std::move(otherobject.s);
        return *this;
    }
};
int main()
{
    MyClass o1{ 123, "This is currently in object 1." };
    MyClass o2{ 456, "This is currently in object 2." };
    o2 = std::move(o1); // move assignment operator invoked
    std::cout << "Move assignment operator used.";
}
```

Output:

```
Move assignment operator used.
```

Here, we defined two objects called o1 and o2. Then we try to move the data from object o1 to o2 by assigning an rvalue reference (of object o1) using the std::move(o1) expression to object o2. This invokes the move assignment operator in our object o2. The move assignment operator implementation itself uses the std::move() function to cast each data member to an rvalue reference.

Operator Overloading

Objects of classes can be used in an expression as operands. For example, we can do the following:

```
myobject = otherobject;
myobject + otherobject;
myobject / otherobject;
myobject++;
++myobject;
```

Here, objects of a class are used as operands. To do that, we need to *overload* the operators for complex types such as classes. It is said that we need to overload them to provide a meaningful operation on objects of a class. Some operators can be overloaded for classes; some cannot. We can overload the following operators – arithmetic, binary, boolean, unary, comparison, compound, function, and subscript operators:

```
+ - * / % ^ & | ~ ! = < > == != <= >= += -= *= /= %= ^= &= |= << >> >>= <<=
&& || ++ -- , ->* -> () []
```

Each operator carries its signature and set of rules when overloading for classes. Some operator overloads are implemented as member functions and some as freestanding functions. Let us overload a unary **prefix ++** operator for classes. It is of signature MyClass& operator++():

```
#include <iostream>

class MyClass
{
private:
    int x;
    double d;
public:
    MyClass()
        : x{ 0 }, d{ 0.0 }
    {
    }
    // prefix operator ++
    MyClass& operator++()
    {
        ++x;
        ++d;
        std::cout << "Prefix operator ++ invoked." << '\n';
```

```
        return *this;
    }
};

int main()
{
    MyClass myobject;
    // prefix operator
    ++myobject;
    // the same as:
    myobject.operator++();
}
```

Output:

```
Prefix operator ++ invoked.
Prefix operator ++ invoked.
```

In this example, when invoked in our class, the overloaded prefix increment ++ operator increments each of the member fields by one. We can also invoke an operator by calling .operator***actual_operator_name***(*parameters_if_any*); such as .operator++();.

Operators often depend on each other and can be implemented in terms of other operators. To implement a postfix operator **++**, we will implement it in terms of a prefix operator:

```
#include <iostream>

class MyClass
{
private:
    int x;
    double d;
public:
    MyClass()
        : x{ 0 }, d{ 0.0 }
    {
    }
```

```
    // prefix operator ++
    MyClass& operator++()
    {
        ++x;
        ++d;
        std::cout << "Prefix operator ++ invoked." << '\n';
        return *this;
    }
    // postfix operator ++
    MyClass operator++(int)
    {
        MyClass tmp(*this); // create a copy
        operator++();       // invoke the prefix operator overload
        std::cout << "Postfix operator ++ invoked." << '\n';
        return tmp;         // return old value
    }
};

int main()
{
    MyClass myobject;
    // postfix operator
    myobject++;
    // is the same as if we had:
    myobject.operator++(0);
}
```

Output:

```
Prefix operator ++ invoked.
Postfix operator ++ invoked.
Prefix operator ++ invoked.
Postfix operator ++ invoked.
```

Please do not worry too much about the somewhat *inconsistent* rules for operator overloading. Remember, each (set of) operator has its own rules for overloading.

Let us overload a binary operator **+=**:

```cpp
#include <iostream>

class MyClass
{
private:
    int x;
    double d;
public:
    MyClass(int xx, double dd)
        : x{ xx }, d{ dd }
    {
    }
    MyClass& operator+=(const MyClass& rhs)
    {
        this->x += rhs.x;
        this->d += rhs.d;
        return *this;
    }
};

int main()
{
    MyClass myobject{ 1, 1.0 };
    MyClass mysecondobject{ 2, 2.0 };
    myobject += mysecondobject;
    std::cout << "Used the overloaded += operator.";
}
```

Output:

```
Used the overloaded += operator.
```

Now, myobject member field x has a value of 3, and member field d has a value of 3.0.

Let us implement the arithmetic **+** operator in terms of the **+=** operator:

```cpp
#include <iostream>

class MyClass
{
private:
    int x;
    double d;
public:
    MyClass(int xx, double dd)
        : x{ xx }, d{ dd }
    {
    }
    MyClass& operator+=(const MyClass& rhs)
    {
        this->x += rhs.x;
        this->d += rhs.d;
        return *this;
    }
    friend MyClass operator+(MyClass lhs, const MyClass& rhs)
    {
        lhs += rhs;
        return lhs;
    }
};

int main()
{
    MyClass myobject{ 1, 1.0 };
    MyClass mysecondobject{ 2, 2.0 };
    MyClass myresult = myobject + mysecondobject;
    std::cout << "Used the overloaded + operator.";
}
```

Output:

```
Used the overloaded + operator.
```

When we need to perform arithmetic, logic, and other operations on our objects of a class, we need to overload the appropriate operators. There are rules and signatures for overloading each operator. Some operators can be implemented in terms of other operators.

We do not have to learn all the operator overloading rules by heart. We should simply look them up. For a complete list of operator overloading rules, please refer to the C++ reference at: `https://en.cppreference.com/w/cpp/language/operators`.

Destructors

As we saw earlier, a constructor is a member function that gets invoked when the object is initialized. Similarly, a destructor is a member function that gets invoked when an object is destroyed. The signature of the destructor starts with a tilde ~ followed by a class name:

```
class MyClass
{
public:
    MyClass() {}    // constructor
    ~MyClass() {}   // destructor
};
```

A destructor takes no parameters, and there is one destructor per class. Example:

```
#include <iostream>

class MyClass
{
public:
    MyClass() {}    // constructor
```

```
    ~MyClass()
    {
        std::cout << "Destructor invoked.";
    }    // destructor
};

int main()
{
    MyClass o;
}   // destructor invoked here when o gets out of scope
```

Output:

```
Destructor invoked.
```

Destructors are invoked when an object goes out of scope or when a pointer to an object is deleted. We should not call the destructor directly.

Destructors can be used to clean up the allocated resources. Example:

```cpp
#include <iostream>

class MyClass
{
private:
    int* p;
public:
    MyClass()
        : p{ new int{123} }
    {
        std::cout << "Created a pointer in the constructor." << '\n';
    }
    ~MyClass()
    {
        delete p;
        std::cout << "Deleted a pointer in the destructor." << '\n';
    }
};
```

```
int main()
{
    MyClass o; // constructor invoked here
} // destructor invoked here
```

Output:

```
Created a pointer in the constructor.
Deleted a pointer in the destructor.
```

Here, we allocate memory for a pointer in the constructor and deallocate the memory in the destructor. This style of resource allocation/deallocation is called RAII or Resource Acquisition Is Initialization. Destructors should not be called directly.

Important   The use of new and delete, as well as the use of raw pointers in modern C++, is **discouraged**. We should use **smart pointers** instead.

We will talk about them later in the book. Let us do some exercises for the class's introductory part.

CHAPTER 24

Exercises

Class Instance

Write a program that defines an empty class called *MyClass* and makes an instance of *MyClass* in the main function.

```
class MyClass
{
};

int main()
{
    MyClass o;
}
```

Class with Data Members

Write a program that defines a class called *MyClass* with three data members of type char, int, and bool. Make an instance of that class inside the main function.

```
class MyClass
{
    char c;
    int x;
    bool b;
};
```

© Slobodan Dmitrović 2023
S. Dmitrović, *Modern C++ for Absolute Beginners*, https://doi.org/10.1007/978-1-4842-9274-7_24

```
int main()
{
    MyClass o;
}
```

Class with Member Function

Write a program that defines a class called MyClass with one member function called printmessage(). Define the printmessage() member function inside the class and have it output the "Hello World" message. Create an instance of that class and use the object to call the class member function.

```
#include <iostream>

class MyClass
{
public:
    void printmessage()
    {
        std::cout << "Hello World.";
    }
};

int main()
{
    MyClass o;
    o.printmessage();
}
```

   Output:

```
Hello World.
```

Class with Data and Function Members

Write a program that defines a class called MyClass with one member function called printmessage(). Define the printmessage() member function outside the class and have it output the "Hello World." string. Create an instance of that class and use the object to call the member function.

```
#include <iostream>

class MyClass
{
public:
    void printmessage();
};

void MyClass::printmessage()
{
    std::cout << "Hello World.";
}

int main()
{
    MyClass o;
    o.printmessage();
}
```

Output:

```
Hello World.
```

Class Access Specifiers

Write a program that defines a class called MyClass with one private data member of type int called x and two member functions. The first member function called setx(int myvalue) will set the value of x to its parameter myvalue. The second member function is called getx(), is of type int, and returns a value of x. Create an instance of the class and use the object to access both member functions.

```
#include <iostream>

class MyClass
{
private:
    int x;
public:
    void setx(int myvalue)
    {
        x = myvalue;
    }
    int getx()
    {
        return x;
    }
};

int main()
{
    MyClass o;
    o.setx(123);
    std::cout << "The value of x is: " << o.getx();
}
```

   Output:

```
The value of x is: 123
```

User-Defined Default Constructor and Destructor

Write a program that defines a class called MyClass with a user-defined default constructor and user-defined destructor. Define both constructor and destructor outside the class body. Both member functions will output a free-to-choose text on the standard output. Create an object of a class in function main.

```
#include <iostream>

class MyClass
{
public:
    MyClass();
    ~MyClass();
};

MyClass::MyClass()
{
    std::cout << "Constructor invoked." << '\n';
}

MyClass::~MyClass()
{
    std::cout << "Destructor invoked." << '\n';
}

int main()
{
    MyClass o;
}
```

   Output:

```
Constructor invoked.
Destructor invoked.
```

Constructor Initializer List

Write a program that defines a class called MyClass, with two private data members of type int and double. Outside the class, define a user-provided constructor accepting two parameters. The constructor initializes both data members with arguments using the initializer. Outside the class, define a function called printdata() which prints the values of both data members.

```cpp
#include <iostream>

class MyClass
{
private:
    int x;
    double d;
public:
    MyClass(int xx, double dd);
    void printdata();
};

MyClass::MyClass(int xx, double dd)
    : x{ xx }, d{ dd }
{
}

void MyClass::printdata()
{
    std::cout << "The value of x: " << x << ", the value of d: " << d
    << '\n';
}

int main()
{
    MyClass o{ 123, 456.789 };
    o.printdata();
}
```

Output:

The value of x: 123, the value of d: 456.789

User-Defined Copy Constructor

Write a program that defines a class called MyClass with arbitrary data fields. Write a user-defined constructor with parameters that initializes data members. Write a user-defined copy constructor which copies all the members. Create one object of the class, called *o1*, and initialize it with values. Create another object of a class, called *o2*, and initialize it with object *o1*. Print out the data for both objects.

```cpp
#include <iostream>

class MyClass
{
private:
    int x;
    double d;
public:
    MyClass(int xx, double dd);      // user-provided constructor
    MyClass(const MyClass& rhs);     // user-defined copy constructor
    void printdata();
};

MyClass::MyClass(int xx, double dd)
    : x{ xx }, d{ dd }
{}

MyClass::MyClass(const MyClass& rhs)
    : x{ rhs.x }, d{ rhs.d }
{}

void MyClass::printdata()
{
    std::cout << "The x is: " << x << ", and the d is: " << d << '\n';
}
```

```
int main()
{
    MyClass o1{ 123, 456.789 }; // invokes a user-provided constructor
    MyClass o2 = o1; // invokes a user-defined copy constructor
    o1.printdata();
    o2.printdata();
}
```

Output:

```
The x is: 123, and the d is: 456.789
The x is: 123, and the d is: 456.789
```

User-Defined Move Constructor

Write a program that defines a class with two data members, a user-provided constructor, a user-provided move constructor, and a member function that prints the data. Invoke the move constructor in the main program. Print the moved-to object data fields.

```
#include <iostream>
#include <string>

class MyClass
{
private:
    double d;
    std::string s;
public:
    MyClass(double dd, std::string ss) // user-provided constructor
        : d{ dd }, s{ ss }
    {}

    MyClass(MyClass&& otherobject) // user-defined move constructor
        :
        d{ std::move(otherobject.d) }, s{ std::move(otherobject.s) }
```

```
    {
        std::cout << "Move constructor invoked." << '\n';
    }

    void printdata()
    {
        std::cout << "The value of a double is: " << d << ", and the value
        of a string is: " << s << '\n';
    }
};

int main()
{
    MyClass o1{ 3.14, "This was in object 1." };
    MyClass o2 = std::move(o1); // invokes the move constructor
    o2.printdata();
}
```

Output:

```
Move constructor invoked.
The value of a double is: 3.14, and the value of a string is: This was in
object 1.
```

Overloading Arithmetic Operators

Write a program that overloads the arithmetic operator – in terms of a compound arithmetic operator -=. Subtract one object from the other and assign the result to a third object. Print out the values of the resulting object's member fields.

```
#include <iostream>

class MyClass
{
private:
    int x;
    double d;
```

```cpp
public:
    MyClass(int xx, double dd)
        : x{ xx }, d{ dd }
    {
    }

    void printvalues()
    {
        std::cout << "The values of x is: " << x << ", the value of d
        is: " << d;
    }

    MyClass& operator-=(const MyClass& rhs)
    {
        this->x -= rhs.x;
        this->d -= rhs.d;
        return *this;
    }

    friend MyClass operator-(MyClass lhs, const MyClass& rhs)
    {
        lhs -= rhs;
        return lhs;
    }
};

int main()
{
    MyClass myobject{ 3, 3.0 };
    MyClass mysecondobject{ 1, 1.0 };
    MyClass myresult = myobject - mysecondobject;
    myresult.printvalues();
}
```

Output:

The values of x is: 2, the value of d is: 2

CHAPTER 25

Classes – Inheritance and Polymorphism

In this chapter, we discuss some of the fundamental building blocks of object-oriented programming, such as inheritance and polymorphism.

Inheritance

We can build a class from an existing class. It is said that a class can be *derived* from an existing class. This is known as *inheritance* and is one of the pillars of object-oriented programming, abbreviated as OOP. To derive a class from an existing class, we write:

```
class MyDerivedClass : public MyBaseClass {};
```

A simple example would be

```
class MyBaseClass
{
};

class MyDerivedClass : public MyBaseClass
{
};

int main()
{
}
```

147

© Slobodan Dmitrović 2023
S. Dmitrović, *Modern C++ for Absolute Beginners*, https://doi.org/10.1007/978-1-4842-9274-7_25

In this example, MyDerivedClass *inherits* the MyBaseClass.

Let us get the terminology out of the way. It is said that MyDerivedClass *is derived* from MyBaseClass, or MyBaseClass is a *base class* for MyDerivedClass. It is also said that MyDerivedClass *is* MyBaseClass. They all mean the same thing.

Now the two classes have some sort of *relationship*. This relationship can be expressed through different naming conventions, but the most important one is *inheritance*. The derived class and objects of a derived class can access public members of a base class:

```cpp
class MyBaseClass
{
public:
    char c;
    int x;
};

class MyDerivedClass : public MyBaseClass
{
    // c and x also accessible here
};

int main()
{
    MyDerivedClass o;
    o.c = 'a';
    o.x = 123;
}
```

The following example introduces the new access specifier called protected:. The derived class itself can access protected members of a base class. The protected access specifier allows access to the base class and derived class but not to objects:

```cpp
class MyBaseClass
{
protected:
    char c;
    int x;
};
```

```
class MyDerivedClass : public MyBaseClass
{
    // c and x also accessible here
};

int main()
{
    MyDerivedClass o;
    o.c = 'a';    // Error, not accessible to an object
    o.x = 123;    // error, not accessible to an object
}
```

The derived class cannot access private members of a base class:

```
class MyBaseClass
{
private:
    char c;
    int x;
};

class MyDerivedClass : public MyBaseClass
{
    // c and x NOT accessible here
};

int main()
{
    MyDerivedClass o;
    o.c = 'a';    // Error, not accessible to object
    o.x = 123;    // error, not accessible to object
}
```

The derived class inherits `public` and `protected` base class members and can introduce its own new members. Here's a simple example:

```cpp
class MyBaseClass
{
public:
    char c;
    int x;
};

class MyDerivedClass : public MyBaseClass
{
public:
    double d;
};

int main()
{
    MyDerivedClass o;
    o.c = 'a';
    o.x = 123;
    o.d = 456.789;
}
```

Here, we inherited everything from the `MyBaseClass` class and introduced a new member field in `MyDerivedClass` called d. So, with `MyDerivedClass`, we are extending the capability of `MyBaseClass`. The field d only exists in `MyDerivedClass` and is accessible to the derived class and its objects. It is not accessible to `MyBaseClass` class as it does not exist there.

Please note that there are other ways of inheriting a class, such as through protected and private inheritance, but the public inheritance, such as `class MyDerivedClass : public MyBaseClass`, is the most widely used, and we will stick to that one for now.

A derived class itself can be a base class. Example:

```cpp
class MyBaseClass
{
public:
    char c;
    int x;
};
```

```
class MyDerivedClass : public MyBaseClass
{
public:
    double d;
};

class MySecondDerivedClass : public MyDerivedClass
{
public:
    bool b;
};

int main()
{
    MySecondDerivedClass o;
    o.c = 'a';
    o.x = 123;
    o.d = 456.789;
    o.b = true;
}
```

Now our class has everything MyDerivedClass has, which includes everything MyBaseClass has, plus an additional bool field. It is said that inheritance produces a particular *hierarchy* of classes.

This approach is widely used when we want to extend the functionality of our classes.

The derived class is compatible with a base class. A pointer to a derived class is compatible with a pointer to a base class. This allows us to utilize *polymorphism*, which we will talk about in the next chapter.

Polymorphism

It is said that the derived class *is* a base class. Its type is compatible with the base class type. Also, a pointer to a derived class is compatible with a pointer to the base class. This is important, so let's repeat this: a pointer to a derived class is compatible with a pointer to a base class. Together with inheritance, this is used to achieve the functionality known as polymorphism. Polymorphism means the object can morph into different types.

Polymorphism in C++ is achieved through an interface known as *virtual functions.* A virtual function is a function whose behavior can be *overridden* in subsequent derived classes. And our pointer/object *morphs* into different types to invoke the appropriate function. Example:

```cpp
#include <iostream>

class MyBaseClass
{
public:
    virtual void dowork()
    {
        std::cout << "Hello from a base class." << '\n';
    }
};

class MyDerivedClass : public MyBaseClass
{
public:
    void dowork()
    {
        std::cout << "Hello from a derived class." << '\n';
    }
};

int main()
{
    MyBaseClass* o = new MyDerivedClass;
    o->dowork();
    delete o;
}
```

  Output:

```
Hello from a derived class.
```

In this example, we have a simple inheritance where MyDerivedClass is derived from MyBaseClass.

The MyBaseClass class has a function called dowork() with a virtual specifier. Virtual means this function can be overridden/redefined in subsequent derived classes, and the appropriate version will be invoked through a polymorphic object. The derived class has a function with the same name and the same type of arguments (none in our case, for now) in the derived class.

In our main program, we create an instance of a MyDerivedClass class **through** a base class pointer. Using the arrow operator ->, we invoke the appropriate version of the function. The -> (arrow) operator does two things: it dereferences a pointer to an object and accesses the member of a class. Here, the o object *morphs* into different types to invoke the appropriate function. Here, it invokes the derived version. That is why the concept is called *polymorphism.*

If there were no dowork() function in the derived class, it would invoke the base class version:

```cpp
#include <iostream>

class MyBaseClass
{
public:
    virtual void dowork()
    {
        std::cout << "Hello from a base class." << '\n';
    }
};

class MyDerivedClass : public MyBaseClass
{
};

int main()
{
    MyBaseClass* o = new MyDerivedClass;
    o->dowork();
    delete o;
}
```

Output:

```
Hello from a base class.
```

Functions can be *pure virtual* by specifying the = 0; at the end of the function declaration. Pure virtual functions do not have definitions and are also called interfaces. Pure virtual functions must be redefined in the derived class. Classes having at least one pure virtual function are called *abstract classes* and cannot be instantiated. They can only be used as base classes. Example:

```cpp
#include <iostream>

class MyAbstractClass
{
public:
    virtual void dowork() = 0;
};

class MyDerivedClass : public MyAbstractClass
{
public:
    void dowork()
    {
        std::cout << "Hello from a derived class." << '\n';
    }
};

int main()
{
    MyAbstractClass* o = new MyDerivedClass;
    o->dowork();
    delete o;
}
```

Output:

```
Hello from a derived class.
```

One important thing to add is that a base class must have a `virtual` destructor if it is to be used in a polymorphic scenario. This ensures the proper deallocation of objects accessed through a base class pointer via the inheritance chain:

```
class MyBaseClass
{
public:
    virtual void dowork() = 0;
    virtual ~MyBaseClass() {};
};
```

Please remember that the use of operator *new* and raw pointers is discouraged in modern C++. We should use smart pointers instead. More on this later in the book.

So, the three pillars of object-oriented programming are

- Encapsulation

- Inheritance

- Polymorphism

Encapsulation is grouping the fields into different visibility zones, hiding implementation from the user, and exposing the interface, for example.

Inheritance is a mechanism where we can create classes by inheriting from a base class. Inheritance creates a certain class hierarchy and relationship between them.

Polymorphism is an ability of an object to morph into different types during runtime, ensuring the proper function is invoked. This is achieved through inheritance, virtual and overridden functions, and base and derived class pointers.

CHAPTER 26

Exercises

Inheritance

Write a program that defines a base class called Person. The class has the following members:

- A data member of type *std::string* called the *name*

- A single-parameter, user-defined constructor which initializes the *name*

- A getter function of type *std::string* called *getname()*, which returns the *name's* value

Then, write a class called *Student*, which inherits from the class *Person*. The class *Student* has the following members:

- An integer data member called the *semester*

- A user-provided constructor that initializes the *name* and *semester* fields

- A getter function of type *int* called *getsemester()*, which returns the *semester's* value

In a nutshell, we have a base class *Person*, and we extend its functionality in the derived *Student* class:

```
#include <iostream>
#include <string>

class Person
{
private:
    std::string name;
```

© Slobodan Dmitrović 2023
S. Dmitrović, *Modern C++ for Absolute Beginners*, https://doi.org/10.1007/978-1-4842-9274-7_26

```cpp
public:
    explicit Person(const std::string& aname)
        : name{ aname }
    {}

    std::string getname() const { return name; }
};

class Student : public Person
{
private:
    int semester;
public:
    Student(const std::string& aname, int asemester)
        : Person::Person{ aname }, semester{ asemester }
    {}

    int getsemester() const { return semester; }
};

int main()
{
    Person person{ "John Doe." };
    std::cout << person.getname() << '\n';
    Student student{ "Jane Doe.", 2 };
    std::cout << student.getname() << '\n';
    std::cout << "The semester is: " << student.getsemester() << '\n';
}
```

Output:

```
John Doe.
Jane Doe.
The semester is: 2
```

Explanation:

We have two classes: one is a base class (Person), and the other (Student) is a derived class. Single-parameter constructors should be marked with `explicit` to prevent the compiler from making implicit conversions. This is the case with *Person*'s user-provided, single-parameter constructor:

```
explicit Person(const std::string& aname)
      : name{ aname }
  {}
```

Member functions that do not modify the member fields should be marked as *const*. The const modifier in member functions promises the functions will not modify the data members and are easier for the compiler to optimize the code. This is the case with both *getname()*:

```
std::string getname() const { return name; }
```

and *getsemester()* member functions:

```
int getsemester() const { return semester; }
```

The *Student* class inherits from the *Person* class and adds additional data field *semester* and member function *getsemester()*. The *Student* class has everything a base class has, plus it extends the functionality of a base class by adding new fields. The *Student*'s user-provided constructor uses the base class constructor in its initializer list to initialize a name field:

```
Student(const std::string& aname, int asemester)
      : Person::Person{ aname }, semester{ asemester }
  {}
```

In the main() program, we instantiate both classes:

```
Person person{ "John Doe." };
```

and

```
Student student{ "Jane Doe", 2 };
```

And call their member functions:

```
person.getname();
```

and

```
student.getname();
student.getsemester();
```

Important   We will make a polymorphism exercise later in the book when we cover the smart pointers. This is because we want to depart from the use of new and `delete` and raw pointers.

CHAPTER 27

The static Specifier

The static specifier says the object will have a *static storage duration*. The memory space for static objects is allocated when the program starts and deallocated when the program ends. Only one instance of a static object exists in the program. If a local variable is marked as static, the space for it is allocated the first time the program control encounters its definition and deallocated when the program exits.

To define a local static variable inside a function, we use:

```cpp
#include <iostream>

void myfunction()
{
    static int x = 0; // defined only the first time, skipped every
    other // time
    x++;
    std::cout << "Function ran: " << x << " time(s)." << '\n';
}

int main()
{
    myfunction(); // x == 1
    myfunction(); // x == 2
    myfunction(); // x == 3
}
```

Output:

```
Function ran: 1 time(s).
Function ran: 2 time(s).
Function ran: 3 time(s).
```

© Slobodan Dmitrović 2023
S. Dmitrović, *Modern C++ for Absolute Beginners*, https://doi.org/10.1007/978-1-4842-9274-7_27

This variable is initialized the first time the program encounters this function. The value of this variable is preserved across function calls. What does this mean? The last changes we made to it *stay*. It will not get initialized to zero for every function call, only the first time.

This is convenient as we do not have to store the value inside some global variable x.

We can define static class member fields. Static class members are not part of the object. They live independently of an object of a class. We declare a static data member inside the class and define it outside the class only once:

```cpp
#include <iostream>

class MyClass
{
public:
    static int x; // declare a static data member
};

int MyClass::x = 123; // define a static data member

int main()
{
    MyClass::x = 456; // access a static data member
    std::cout << "Static data member value is: " << MyClass::x;
}
```

Output:

```
Static data member value is: 456
```

Here, we declared a static data member inside a class. Then we defined it outside the class. When defining a static member outside the class, we do not need to use the static specifier. Then, we access the data member by using the MyClass::data_member_name notation.

To define a static member function, we prepend the function declaration with the *static* keyword. The function definition outside the class does not use the *static* keyword:

```cpp
#include <iostream>

class MyClass
{
public:
    static void myfunction(); // declare a static member function
};

// define a static member function
void MyClass::myfunction()
{
    std::cout << "Hello World from a static member function.";
}

int main()
{
    MyClass::myfunction(); // call a static member function
}
```

Output:

Hello World from a static member function.

CHAPTER 28

Templates

Templates are mechanisms to support the so-called *generic programming*. Generic broadly means we can define a function or a class without worrying about what types it accepts.

We define those functions and classes using some generic type. And when we instantiate them, we use a concrete type. So, we can use templates when we want to define a class or a function that can accept almost any type.

We define a template by typing

```
template <typename T>
// the rest of our function or class code
```

which is the same as if we used

```
template <class T>
// the rest of our function or class code
```

T here stands for a type name. Which type? Well, any type. Here, T means *for all types T*.

Function Templates

Using template functionality, we can create function templates that can accept any type.

Let us create a function that can accept an argument of any type:

```
#include <iostream>

template <typename T>
void myfunction(T param)
{
    std::cout << "The value of a parameter is: " << param;
}
```

© Slobodan Dmitrović 2023
S. Dmitrović, *Modern C++ for Absolute Beginners*, https://doi.org/10.1007/978-1-4842-9274-7_28

```
int main()
{
}
```

To instantiate a function template, we call a function by supplying a specific type name surrounded by angle brackets:

```
#include <iostream>

template <typename T>
void myfunction(T param)
{
    std::cout << "The value of a parameter is: " << param << '\n';
}

int main()
{
    myfunction<int>(123);
    myfunction<double>(123.456);
    myfunction<char>('A');
}
```

Output:

```
The value of a parameter is: 123
The value of a parameter is: 123.456
The value of a parameter is: A
```

We can think of T as a placeholder for a specific type, the one we supply when we instantiate a template. So, in place of T, we now put our specific type. This way, we can utilize the same code for different types.

Templates can have more than one parameter. We list the template parameters and separate them using a comma. Here's an example of a function template that accepts two template parameters:

```
#include <iostream>

template <typename T, typename U>
void myfunction(T t, U u)
```

```
{
    std::cout << "The first parameter is: " << t << '\n';
    std::cout << "The second parameter is: " << u << '\n';
}

int main()
{
    int x = 123;
    double d = 456.789;
    myfunction<int, double>(x, d);
}
```

Output:

```
The first parameter is: 123
The second parameter is: 456.789
```

Class Templates

Using templates, we can also create *class templates*, which are basically classes that can have data members of any type, member functions, and member functions' arguments of any type.

To define a simple class template, we use the following approach:

```
#include <iostream>

template <typename T>
class MyClass {
private:
    T x;
public:
    MyClass(T xx)
        :x{ xx }
    {
    }
```

```
    T getvalue()
    {
        return x;
    }
};

int main()
{
    MyClass<int> o{ 123 };
    std::cout << "The value of x is: " << o.getvalue() << '\n';
    MyClass<double> o2{ 456.789 };
    std::cout << "The value of x is: " << o2.getvalue() << '\n';
}
```

Output:

```
The value of x is: 123
The value of x is: 456.789
```

Here, we defined a simple class template. The class accepts generic type T, meaning it can accept any given type at the point of instantiation, which happens in our function main. We use those types wherever we find appropriate in our class. In our main function, we instantiate those classes with concrete types int and double. Instead of writing the same code for two or more different types, we use a template.

To define class template member functions outside the class, we need to make them templates themselves by prepending the member function definition with the appropriate template declaration. In such definitions, a class name must be called with a template argument. Here's a simple example:

```
#include <iostream>

template <typename T>
class MyClass {
private:
    T x;
public:
    MyClass(T xx);
};
```

```
template <typename T>
MyClass<T>::MyClass(T xx)
    : x{xx}
{
    std::cout << "Constructor invoked. The value of x is: " << x << '\n';
}

int main()
{
    MyClass<int> o{ 123 };
    MyClass<double> o2{ 456.789 };
}
```

Output:

```
Constructor invoked. The value of x is: 123
Constructor invoked. The value of x is: 456.789
```

Let us make it simpler. If we had a class template with a single void member function, we would write

```
template <typename T>
class MyClass {
public:
    void somefunction();
};

template <typename T>
void MyClass<T>::somefunction()
{
    // function implementation
}
```

If we had a class template with a single member function of type T, we would use

```
template <typename T>
class MyClass {
public:
    T genericfunction();
};

template <typename T>
T MyClass<T>::genericfunction()
{
    // function implementation
}
```

Now, if we had both of them in a single class and we wanted to define both of them outside the class scope, we would use the following:

```
template <typename T>
class MyClass {
public:
    void somefunction();
    T genericfunction();
};

template <typename T>
void MyClass<T>::somefunction()
{
    // the rest of the code
}

template <typename T>
T MyClass<T>::genericfunction()
{
    // the rest of the code
}
```

Template Specialization

If we want our template to behave differently, only for a specific type, we provide the so-called *template specialization*. Let us say we want our class template to behave differently only in case an *int* type was used. To do that, first, we prepend our function or class with the following:

```
template <>
// the rest of our template code
```

To specialize our template function for type *int*, we write

```
#include <iostream>

template <typename T>
void myfunction(T arg)
{
    std::cout << "The value of an argument is: " << arg << '\n';
}

template <>
// the template specialization code follows
void myfunction(int arg)
{
    std::cout << "This is a specialization for an int. The value is: "
    << arg << '\n';
}

int main()
{
    myfunction<char>('A');
    myfunction<double>(345.678);
    myfunction<int>(123); // invokes specialization
}
```

Output:

The value of an argument is: A
The value of an argument is: 345.678
This is a specialization for an int. The value is: 123

CHAPTER 29

Enumerations

Enumeration, or *enum* for short, is a type whose values are symbolic, user-defined, named constants called *enumerators*.

There are two kinds of enums: the *unscoped enums* and *scoped enums*. The unscoped enum type can be defined with

```
enum MyEnum
{
    myfirstvalue,
    mysecondvalue,
    mythirdvalue
};
```

To declare a variable of enumeration type MyEnum, we write

```
enum MyEnum
{
    myfirstvalue,
    mysecondvalue,
    mythirdvalue
};
int main()
{
    MyEnum myenum = myfirstvalue;
    myenum = mysecondvalue; // we can change the value of our enum object
}
```

© Slobodan Dmitrović 2023

S. Dmitrović, *Modern C++ for Absolute Beginners*, https://doi.org/10.1007/978-1-4842-9274-7_29

Each enumerator has a value of the underlying type. We can change those:

```
enum MyEnum
{
    myfirstvalue = 10,
    mysecondvalue,
    mythirdvalue
};
```

These unscoped enums have their enumerators *leak* into an outside scope, the scope in which the enum type itself is defined. Old enums are best avoided. Prefer *scoped enums* to unscoped enums, as scoped enums do not leak their enumerators into an outer scope and are not implicitly convertible to other types. To define a scoped enum, we write

```
enum class MyEnum
{
    myfirstvalue,
    mysecondvalue,
    mythirdvalue
};
```

To declare a variable of type enum class (scoped enum), we write

```
enum class MyEnum
{
    myfirstvalue,
    mysecondvalue,
    mythirdvalue
};
int main()
{
    MyEnum myenum = MyEnum::myfirstvalue;
}
```

To access an enumerator value, we prepend the enumerator with the enum name and a scope resolution operator :: such as MyEnum::myfirstvalue, MyEnum::mysecondvalue, etc.

With these enums, the enumerator names are defined only within the enum's internal scope and do not implicitly convert to underlying types. We can specify the underlying type for the scoped enum:

```
enum class MyCharEnum : char
{
    myfirstvalue,
    mysecondvalue,
    mythirdvalue
};
```

We can also change the initial underlying values of enumerators by specifying the value:

```
enum class MyEnum
{
    myfirstvalue = 15,
    mysecondvalue,
    mythirdvalue = 30
};
```

Prefer enum class enumerations (scoped enums) to old, plain, unscoped enums. Use enumerations to represent states, for example, when our object can have one value out of a set of predefined named values.

CHAPTER 30

Exercises

Static Variable

Write a program that checks how many times a function was called from the main program. We will use a local static variable inside a function, and we will increment this variable each time the function is called in main():

```cpp
#include <iostream>

void myfunction()
{
    static int counter = 0;
    counter++;
    std::cout << "The function is called " << counter << " time(s)."
    << '\n';
}

int main()
{
    myfunction();
    myfunction();
    for (int i = 0; i < 5; i++)
    {
        myfunction();
    }
}
```

© Slobodan Dmitrović 2023
S. Dmitrović, *Modern C++ for Absolute Beginners*, https://doi.org/10.1007/978-1-4842-9274-7_30

Output:

```
The function is called 1 time(s).
The function is called 2 time(s).
The function is called 3 time(s).
The function is called 4 time(s).
The function is called 5 time(s).
The function is called 6 time(s).
The function is called 7 time(s).
```

Static Data Member

Write a program that defines a class with one static data member of type std::string. Make the data member public. Then, define this static data member outside the class. Change the static data member's value from the main function:

```cpp
#include <iostream>
#include <string>

class MyClass
{
public:
    static std::string name;
};

std::string MyClass::name = "John Doe";

int main()
{
    std::cout << "Static data member value: " << MyClass::name << '\n';
    MyClass::name = "Jane Doe";
    std::cout << "Static data member value: " << MyClass::name << '\n';
}
```

Output:

```
Static data member value: John Doe
Static data member value: Jane Doe
```

Static Member Function

Write a program that defines a class with one static member function and one regular, nonstatic member function. Make both functions public. Define both member functions outside the class. Invoke both functions from the main program:

```cpp
#include <iostream>
#include <string>

class MyClass
{
public:
    static void mystaticfunction();
    void myfunction();
};

void MyClass::mystaticfunction()
{
    std::cout << "Hello World from a static member function." << '\n';
}

void MyClass::myfunction()
{
    std::cout << "Hello World from a regular member function." << '\n';
}

int main()
{
    MyClass::mystaticfunction();
    MyClass myobject;
    myobject.myfunction();
}
```

Output:

```
Hello World from a static member function.
Hello World from a regular member function.
```

Function Template

Write a program that defines a template for a function that sums two numbers. Numbers are of the same generic type, T, and are passed to the function as arguments. Instantiate the function in the main program using types int and double:

```cpp
#include <iostream>

template <typename T>
T mysum(T x, T y)
{
    return x + y;
}

int main()
{
    int intresult = mysum<int>(10, 20);
    std::cout << "The integer sum result is: " << intresult << '\n';
    double doubleresult = mysum<double>(123.456, 789.101);
    std::cout << "The double sum result is: " << doubleresult << '\n';
}
```

Output:

```
The integer sum result is: 30
The double sum result is: 912.557
```

Class Template

Write a program that defines a simple class template with one data member of a generic type, a constructor, a getter function of a generic type, and a setter member function. Instantiate the class template in the main function using types int and double:

```cpp
#include <iostream>

template <typename T>
class MyClass
{
private:
    T x;
public:
    MyClass(T xx)
        : x{ xx }
    {}

    T getx() const
    {
        return x;
    }

    void setx(T ax)
    {
        . x = ax;
    }
};

int main()
{
    MyClass<int> o{123};
    std::cout << "The value of the data member is: " << o.getx() << '\n';
    o.setx(456);
    std::cout << "The value of the data member is: " << o.getx() << '\n';
    MyClass<double> o2{ 4.25 };
```

```
    std::cout << "The value of the data member is: " << o2.getx() << '\n';
    o2.setx(6.28);
    std::cout << "The value of the data member is: " << o2.getx() << '\n';
}
```

Output:

```
The value of the data member is: 123
The value of the data member is: 456
The value of the data member is: 4.25
The value of the data member is: 6.28
```

Scoped Enums

Write a program that defines a scoped enum representing days of the week. Create an object of that enum, assign it a value, and check if it is *Monday*. If it is, change the object's value to another enum value:

```cpp
#include <iostream>

enum class Days
{
    Monday,
    Tuesday,
    Wednesday,
    Thursday,
    Friday,
    Saturday,
    Sunday
};

int main()
{
    Days myday = Days::Monday;
    std::cout << "The enum value is now Monday." << '\n';
    if (myday == Days::Monday)
```

```
    {
        myday = Days::Friday;
    }
    std::cout << "The value is now Friday.";
}
```

Output:

```
The enum value is now Monday.
The value is now Friday.
```

Enums in a switch

Write a program that defines an enumerator type. Create an object of that enum and use it in a switch statement. Use the switch statement to print the value of an object:

```cpp
#include <iostream>

enum class Colors
{
    Red,
    Green,
    Blue
};

int main()
{
    Colors mycolors = Colors::Green;
    switch (mycolors)
    {
    case Colors::Red:
        std::cout << "The color is Red." << '\n';
        break;
    case Colors::Green:
        std::cout << "The color is Green." << '\n';
        break;
```

```
    case Colors::Blue:
        std::cout << "The color is Blue." << '\n';
        break;
    default:
        break;
    }
}
```

Output:

The color is Green.

CHAPTER 31

Organizing Code

We can split our C++ code into multiple files. By convention, there are two kinds of files into which we can store our C++ source: *header files* (headers) and *source files*.

Header and Source Files

Header files are source code files where we usually put various declarations. Header files usually have the *.h* (or *.hpp*) extension. Source files are files where we can store our definitions and the main program. They usually have the *.cpp* (or *.cc*) extension.

Then we include the header files into our source files using the #include preprocessor directive. To include a standard library header, we use the #include statement followed by a header name without an extension, enclosed in angled brackets such as <headername>. Example:

```
#include <iostream>
#include <string>
// etc
```

To include user-defined header files, we use the #include statement, followed by a full header name with an extension enclosed in double quotes. Example:

```
#include "myheader.h"
#include "otherheader.h"
// etc
```

The realistic scenario is that sometimes we need to include both standard library headers and user-defined headers:

```
#include <iostream>
#include "myheader.h"
// etc
```

© Slobodan Dmitrović 2023
S. Dmitrović, *Modern C++ for Absolute Beginners*, https://doi.org/10.1007/978-1-4842-9274-7_31

The compiler *stitches* the code from the header file and the source file together and produces what is called a *translation unit*. The compiler then uses this file to create an object file. A linker then links object files together to create an executable program or a library.

We should put the declarations and constants into header files and put definitions and executable code in source files.

Header Guards

Multiple source files might include the same header file. We use a mechanism called *header guards* to ensure that our header is included only once in the compilation process. It ensures that our header content is included only once in the compilation process. We surround the code in our header file with the following macros:

```
#ifndef MY_HEADER_H
#define MY_HEADER_H

// header file source code
// goes here

#endif
```

This approach ensures the code inside a header file is included only once during the compilation phase.

Namespaces

So far, we have seen how to group parts of our C++ code into *headers* and *source files*. There is another way we can logically group parts of our C++ source code, and that is through *namespaces*. A namespace is a scope with a name. To declare a namespace, we write

```
namespace MyNameSpace
{
}
```

To declare, for example, objects inside a namespace, we use

```
namespace MyNameSpace
{
    int x;
    double d;
}
```

To refer to these objects outside the namespace, we use their fully qualified names. This means we use the *namespace_name::our_object* notation. Here's an example where we define the objects outside the namespace they were declared in:

```
namespace MyNameSpace
{
    int x;
    double d;
}

int main()
{
    MyNameSpace::x = 123;
    MyNameSpace::d = 456.789;
}
```

To introduce an entire namespace into the current scope, we can use the using directive:

```
namespace MyNameSpace
{
    int x;
    double d;
}

using namespace MyNameSpace;

int main()
{
    x = 123;
    d = 456.789;
}
```

If we have several separate namespaces with the same name in our code, we are *extending* that namespace, we are not redefining it. Example:

```
namespace MyNameSpace
{
    int x;
    double d;
}

namespace MyNameSpace
{
    char c;
    bool b;
}

int main()
{
    MyNameSpace::x = 123;
    MyNameSpace::d = 456.789;
    MyNameSpace::c = 'a';
    MyNameSpace::b = true;
}
```

We now have x, d, c, and b inside our MyNameSpace namespace. We are *extending* the MyNameSpace, not redefining it.

A namespace can be spread across multiple files, both headers and source files. We will often see production code wrapped into namespaces. It is an excellent mechanism to group the code into namespaces logically.

Two namespaces with different names can hold an object with the same name. Since every namespace is a different scope, they now declare two different, unrelated objects with the same name. It prevents name clashes:

```
#include <iostream>

namespace MyNameSpace
{
    int x;
}
```

```
namespace MySecondNameSpace
{
    int x;
}

int main()
{
    MyNameSpace::x = 123;
    MySecondNameSpace::x = 456;
    std::cout << "The 1st x is: " << MyNameSpace::x << ", the 2nd x is: "
    << MySecondNameSpace::x;
}
```

Output:

```
The 1st x is: 123, the 2nd x is: 456
```

CHAPTER 32

Exercises

Header and Source Files

Write a program that declares an arbitrary function in a header file. The header file is called *myheader.h*. Define this function inside the main program source file called *source.cpp*. The `main` function is also located inside a *source.cpp* file. Include the header into our source file and invoke the function.

The content of the *myheader.h* file:

```
void myfunction();   //function declaration
```

The content of the *source.cpp* file:

```
#include "myheader.h" //include the header
#include <iostream>

int main()
{
    myfunction();
}

// function definition
void myfunction()
{
    std::cout << "Hello World from multiple files.";
}
```

Output:

```
Hello World from multiple files.
```

© Slobodan Dmitrović 2023
S. Dmitrović, *Modern C++ for Absolute Beginners*, https://doi.org/10.1007/978-1-4842-9274-7_32

Multiple Source Files

Write a program that declares an arbitrary function in a header file. The header file is called *mylibrary.h*. Define a function inside the source file called *mylibrary.cpp*. The main function is inside a second source file called the *source.cpp* file. Include the header in both source files and invoke the function.

The content of the *mylibrary.h* file:

```
void myfunction();  //function declaration
```

The content of the *mylibrary.cpp* file:

```
#include "mylibrary.h"
#include <iostream>

// function definition
void myfunction()
{
    std::cout << "Hello World from multiple files.";
}
```

The content of the *source.cpp* file:

```
#include "mylibrary.h"

int main()
{
    myfunction();
}
```

Output:

```
Hello World from multiple files.
```

Explanation:

This program has three files:

- A header file called *mylibrary.h* is where we put our function declaration.

- We put our function definition in a source file called mylibrary.cpp. We include the header file *mylibrary.h* into the *mylibrary.cpp* source file.

- A source file called *source.cpp* is where the main program is. We also include the *mylibrary.h* header file into this source file.

Since our header file is included in multiple source files, we should put header guard macros into it. The *mylibrary.h* file now looks like the following:

```
#ifndef MY_LIBRARY_H
#define MY_LIBRARY_H
void myfunction();
#endif // !MY_LIBRARY_H
```

To compile a program that has multiple source files, with g++, we use

```
g++ source.cpp mylibrary.cpp
```

The Visual Studio IDE organizes multiple source and header files into projects and automatically compiles all the files.

Namespaces

Write a program that declares a function inside a namespace and defines the function outside the namespace. Invoke the function in the main program. Namespace and function names are arbitrary.

```
#include <iostream>

namespace MyNameSpace
{
    void myfunction();
}
```

```
void MyNameSpace::myfunction()
{
    std::cout << "Hello World from a function inside a namespace.";
}

int main()
{
    MyNameSpace::myfunction();
}
```

Output:

```
Hello World from a function inside a namespace.
```

Nested Namespaces

Write a program that defines a namespace called A and another namespace called B, nested inside the namespace A. Declare a function inside the namespace B and define the function outside both namespaces. Invoke the function in the main program. Then, introduce the entire namespace B to the current scope and invoke the function.

```
#include <iostream>

namespace A
{
    namespace B
    {
        void myfunction();
    }
}

void A::B::myfunction()
{
    std::cout << "Hello World from a function inside a nested namespace."
    << '\n';
}
```

```
int main()
{
    A::B::myfunction();
    using namespace A::B;
    myfunction();
}
```

Output:

```
Hello World from a function inside a nested namespace.
Hello World from a function inside a nested namespace.
```

CHAPTER 33

Conversions

Types can be converted to other types. For example, built-in types can be converted to other built-in types. Here, we will discuss the implicit and explicit conversions.

Implicit Conversions

Some values can be implicitly converted into each other. This is true for all the built-in types. We can convert char to int, int to double, etc. Example:

```
int main()
{
    char mychar = 64;
    int myint = 123;
    double mydouble = 456.789;
    bool myboolean = true;
    myint = mychar;
    mydouble = myint;
    mychar = myboolean;
}
```

We can also implicitly convert double to int. However, some information is lost, and the compiler will warn us about this. This is called *narrowing conversions*:

```
int main()
{
    int myint = 123;
    double mydouble = 456.789;
    myint = mydouble; // the decimal part is lost
}
```

197

© Slobodan Dmitrović 2023
S. Dmitrović, *Modern C++ for Absolute Beginners*, https://doi.org/10.1007/978-1-4842-9274-7_33

When *smaller* integer types such as char or short are used in arithmetic operations, they get promoted/converted to integers. This is referred to as *integral promotion*. For example, if we use two chars in an arithmetic operation, both get converted to an integer, and the whole expression is of type int. This conversion happens only inside the arithmetic expression:

```
int main()
{
    char c1 = 10;
    char c2 = 20;
    auto result = c1 + c2; // result is of type int
}
```

Any built-in type can be converted to a boolean. For objects of those types, any value other than zero gets converted to a boolean value of true, and values equal to zero implicitly convert to a value of false. Example:

```
int main()
{
    char mychar = 64;
    int myint = 0;
    double mydouble = 3.14;
    bool myboolean = true;
    myboolean = mychar;     // true
    myboolean = myint;      // false
    myboolean = mydouble;   // true
}
```

Conversely, a boolean type can be converted to int. The value of true converts to an integer value of one, and the value of false converts to an integer value of zero.

A pointer of any type can be converted to void* type. Here's an example where we convert an integer pointer to a void pointer:

```
int main()
{
    int x = 123;
    int* pint = &x;
    void* pvoid = pint;
}
```

While we can convert any data pointer to a void pointer, we cannot dereference the void pointer. To be able to access the object pointed to by a void pointer, we need to cast the void pointer to some other pointer type first. To do that, we can use the explicit cast function static_cast described in the next chapter:

```cpp
#include <iostream>

int main()
{
    int x = 123;
    int* pint = &x;
    void* pvoid = pint; // convert from int pointer
    int* pint2 = static_cast<int*>(pvoid); // cast a void pointer to int
// pointer
    std::cout << *pint2; // dereference a pointer
}
```

Output:

123

Arrays are implicitly convertible to pointers. When we assign an array name to the pointer, the pointer points at the first element in an array. Example:

```cpp
#include <iostream>

int main()
{
    int arr[5] = { 1, 2, 3, 4, 5 };
    int* p = arr; // pointer to the first array element
    std::cout << *p;
}
```

Output:

1

In this case, we have an implicit conversion of type int[] to type int*.

When used as function arguments, the array gets converted to a pointer. More precisely, it gets converted to a pointer to the first element in an array. In such cases, the array loses its dimension, and it is said it *decays* to a pointer. Example:

```
#include <iostream>

void myfunction(int arg[])
{
    std::cout << arg;
}

int main()
{
    int arr[5] = { 1, 2, 3, 4, 5 };
    myfunction(arr);
}
```

Possible Output:

004FFE40

Here, the arr argument gets converted to a pointer to the first element in an array. Since arg is now a pointer, printing it outputs a pointer value similar to the 004FFE40, not the value it points to. To output the value it points to, we need to dereference the pointer:

```
#include <iostream>

void myfunction(int arg[])
{
    std::cout << *arg;
}

int main()
{
    int arr[5] = { 1, 2, 3, 4, 5 };
    myfunction(arr);
}
```

Output:

1

It is important to adopt the following: in modern C++, we **prefer** *std::vector* and *std::array* containers to raw arrays and pointers.

Explicit Conversions

We can explicitly convert the value of one type to another. Let us start with the `static_cast` function. This function converts between implicitly convertible types. A signature of the function is

```
static_cast<type_to_convert_to>(value_to_convert_from)
```

If we want to convert from a `double` to an `int`, we write

```
int main()
{
    auto myinteger = static_cast<int>(123.456);
}
```

Prefer this verbose function to implicit conversions, as the `static_cast` is the idiomatic way of converting between convertible types. This function performs a compile-time conversion.

The following explicit conversion functions should be used **rarely** and carefully. They are `dynamic_cast` and `reinterpret_cast`. The `dynamic_cast` function converts pointers of the base class to pointers to the derived class and vice versa up the inheritance chain. Example:

```
#include <iostream>

class MyBaseClass {
public:
    virtual ~MyBaseClass() {}
};
```

```cpp
class MyDerivedClass : public MyBaseClass {};

int main()
{
    MyBaseClass* base = new MyDerivedClass;
    MyDerivedClass* derived = new MyDerivedClass;
    // base to derived
    if (dynamic_cast<MyDerivedClass*>(base))
    {
        std::cout << "OK. Convertible.\n";
    }
    else
    {
        std::cout << "Not convertible.\n";
    }
    // derived to base
    if (dynamic_cast<MyBaseClass*>(derived))
    {
        std::cout << "OK. Convertible.\n";
    }
    else
    {
        std::cout << "Not convertible.\n";
    }
    delete base;
    delete derived;
}
```

Output:

```
OK. Convertible.
OK. Convertible.
```

If the conversion succeeds, the result is a pointer to a base or derived class, depending on our use case. If the conversion cannot be done, the result is a pointer of value nullptr.

To use this function, our class must be polymorphic, which means our base class should have at least one virtual function. To try to convert some unrelated class to one of our classes in the inheritance chain, we would use the following:

```cpp
#include <iostream>

class MyBaseClass {
public:
    virtual ~MyBaseClass() {}
};

class MyDerivedClass : public MyBaseClass {};

class MyUnrelatedClass {};

int main()
{
    MyBaseClass* base = new MyDerivedClass;
    MyDerivedClass* derived = new MyDerivedClass;
    MyUnrelatedClass* unrelated = new MyUnrelatedClass;
    // base to derived
    if (dynamic_cast<MyUnrelatedClass*>(base))
    {
        std::cout << "OK. Convertible.\n";
    }
    else
    {
        std::cout << "Not convertible.\n";
    }
    // derived to base
    if (dynamic_cast<MyUnrelatedClass*>(derived))
    {
        std::cout << "OK.\n";
    }
    else
    {
        std::cout << "Not convertible.\n";
    }
```

```
    delete base;
    delete derived;
    delete unrelated;
}
```

Output:

```
Not convertible.
Not convertible.
```

This would fail as the dynamic_cast can only convert between related classes inside the inheritance chain. In reality, we would hardly ever have to use dynamic_cast in the real world.

The third and most dangerous cast is reinterpret_cast. This one is best avoided as it does not offer guarantees of any kind. With that in mind, we will skip its description and move on to the next chapter.

Important: The static_cast function is probably the only cast we will be using most of the time.

CHAPTER 34

Exceptions

If an error occurs in our program, we want to be able to handle it in some way. One way to do this is through *exceptions*. Exceptions are mechanisms where we try to execute some code in the try{} block, and if an error occurs, an exception is thrown. The control is then transferred to a catch clause, which handles that exception. A structure of a try/catch block would be:

```cpp
int main()
{
    try
    {
        // your code here
        // throw an exception if there is an error
    }
    catch (type_of_the_exception e)
    {
        // catch and handle the exception
    }
}
```

A simple *try/catch* example would be

```cpp
#include <iostream>

int main()
{
    try
    {
        std::cout << "Let's assume some error occurred in our program."
        << '\n';
        std::cout << "We throw an exception of type int, for example." << '\n';
```

© Slobodan Dmitrović 2023
S. Dmitrović, *Modern C++ for Absolute Beginners*, https://doi.org/10.1007/978-1-4842-9274-7_34

```
        std::cout << "This signals that something went wrong." << '\n';
        throw 123;      // throw an exception if there is an error
    }
    catch (int e)
    {
        // catch and handle the exception
        std::cout << "Exception raised!" << '\n';
        std::cout << "The exception has a value of " << e <<  '\n';
    }
}
```

Output:

```
Let's assume some error occurred in our program.
We throw an exception of type int, for example.
This signals that something went wrong.
Exception raised!
The exception has a value of 123
```

Explanation: Here, we try to execute code inside the try block. If an error occurs, we throw an exception that signals something went wrong. The exception in our case is of type int, but it can be of any type. When the exception is thrown, the control is transferred to a catch clause, which handles the exception. In our case, it handles the exception of type int.

We can throw an exception of a different type, std::string, for example:

```
#include <iostream>
#include <string>

int main()
{
    try
    {
        std::cout << "Let's assume some error occurred in our program."
            << '\n';
        std::cout << "We throw an exception of type string, for example."
            << '\n';
```

```
        std::cout << "This signals that something went wrong." << '\n';
        throw std::string{ "Some string error" };      // throw an exception
        // if there is an error
    }
    catch (const std::string& e)
    {
        // catch and handle the exception
        std::cout << "String exception raised!" << '\n';
        std::cout << "The exception has a value of: " << e << '\n';
    }
}
```

Output:

```
Let's assume some error occurred in our program.
We throw an exception of type string, for example.
This signals that something went wrong.
String exception raised!
The exception has a value of: Some string error
```

We can have/raise multiple exceptions. They can be of different types. In this case, we have one try and multiple catch blocks. Each catch block handles a different exception.

```
#include <iostream>
#include <string>

int main()
{
    try
    {
        throw 123;
        // the following will not execute as
        // the control has been transferred to a catch clause
        throw std::string{ "Some string error" };
    }
```

```cpp
    catch (int e)
    {
        std::cout << "Integer exception raised! The value is "
        << e << '\n';
    }
    catch (const std::string& e)
    {
        // catch and handle the exception
        std::cout << "String exception raised!." << '\n';
        std::cout << "The exception has a value of: " << e << '\n';
    }
}
```

Output:

```
Integer exception raised! The value is 123
```

Here, we throw multiple exceptions in the try block. The first is of type int, and the second is of std::string type. The moment the first exception is thrown, the control of the program is transferred to a catch clause. This means that the remainder of the code inside the try block will not be executed.

A more realistic scenario would be:

```cpp
#include <iostream>
#include <string>

int main()
{
    try
    {
        bool someflag = true;
        bool someotherflag = true;
        std::cout << "We can have multiple throw exceptions." << '\n';
        if (someflag)
        {
            std::cout << "Throwing an int exception." << '\n';
            throw 123;
```

```
        }
        if(someotherflag)
        {
            std::cout << "Throwing a string exception." << '\n';
            throw std::string{ "Some string error" };
        }
    }
    catch (int e)
    {
        // catch and handle the exception
        std::cout << "Integer exception raised!." << '\n';
        std::cout << "The exception has a value of: " << e << '\n';
    }
    catch (const std::string& e)
    {
        // catch and handle the exception
        std::cout << "String exception raised!" << '\n';
        std::cout << "The exception has a value of: " << e << '\n';
    }
}
```

Output:

```
We can have multiple throw exceptions.
Throwing an int exception.
Integer exception raised!
The exception has a value of: 123
```

Here, we are throwing multiple exceptions inside the try block. The control is transferred to an appropriate catch clause when a first exception is encountered.

CHAPTER 35

Smart Pointers

Smart pointers are pointers that own the object they point to and automatically destroy the object they point to and deallocate the memory once the pointers go out of scope. This way, we do not have to manually delete the object, which was the case with the `new` and `delete` operators.

Smart pointers are declared in the `<memory>` header. We will cover the following smart pointers – unique and shared.

Unique Pointer

A unique pointer called `std::unique_ptr` is a pointer that owns an object it points to. The pointer cannot be copied. A unique pointer deletes the object and deallocates memory for it once it goes out of scope. To declare a unique pointer to a simple `int` object, we write

```
#include <iostream>
#include <memory>

int main()
{
    std::unique_ptr<int> p(new int{ 123 });
    std::cout << *p;
}
```

Output:

123

© Slobodan Dmitrović 2023
S. Dmitrović, *Modern C++ for Absolute Beginners*, https://doi.org/10.1007/978-1-4842-9274-7_35

This example creates a pointer to an object of type int and assigns a value of 123 to the object. A unique pointer can be dereferenced in the same way as a regular pointer using the *p notation. The object gets deleted once p goes out of scope, which, in this case, is at the closing brace }. No explicit use of the delete operator is required.

A better way to initialize a unique pointer is through a std::make_unique<some_type>(some_value) function, where we specify the type for the object in angle brackets and the value for the object the pointer points at in parentheses:

```cpp
#include <iostream>
#include <memory>

int main()
{
    std::unique_ptr<int> p = std::make_unique<int>(123);
    std::cout << *p;
}
```

Output:

```
123
```

The std::make_unique function was introduced in the C++14 standard. Make sure to compile with the *-std=c++14* flag to be able to use this function.

We can create a unique pointer that points to an object of a class and then use its -> operator to access object members:

```cpp
#include <iostream>
#include <memory>

class MyClass
{
public:
    void printmessage()
    {
        std::cout << "Hello from a class.";
    }
};
```

```
int main()
{
    std::unique_ptr<MyClass> p = std::make_unique<MyClass>();
    p->printmessage();
}
```

Output:

```
Hello from a class.
```

The object gets destroyed once p goes out of scope. So, prefer a unique pointer to a raw pointer and their new-delete mechanism. Once p goes out of scope, the pointed-to object of a class gets destroyed.

We can utilize polymorphic classes using a unique pointer:

```
#include <iostream>
#include <memory>

class MyBaseClass
{
public:
    virtual void printmessage()
    {
        std::cout << "Hello from a base class.";
    }
};

class MyderivedClass: public MyBaseClass
{
public:
    void printmessage()
    {
        std::cout << "Hello from a derived class.";
    }
};
```

```
int main()
{
    std::unique_ptr<MyBaseClass> p = std::make_unique<MyderivedClass>();
    p->printmessage();
}
```

Output:

```
Hello from a derived class.
```

With smart pointers, there is no need to explicitly delete the allocated memory, the smart pointer does it for us, hence the *smart* part.

Shared Pointer

We can have multiple pointers point to a single object. We can say that all of them own our pointed-to object. That is, our object has *shared ownership*. And our pointed-to object gets deleted only when the last of those pointers get destroyed. This is what a shared pointer is for. Multiple pointers point to a single object, and when all of them get out of scope, the object gets destroyed.

A shared pointer is defined as `std::shared_ptr<some_type>`. It can be initialized using the `std::make_shared<some_type>(some_value)` function. Shared pointers can be copied. To have three shared pointers pointing at the same object, we can write

```
#include <iostream>
#include <memory>

int main()
{
    std::shared_ptr<int> p1 = std::make_shared<int>(123);
    std::shared_ptr<int> p2 = p1;
    std::shared_ptr<int> p3 = p1;
    std::cout << "Shared pointer 1 points at: " << *p1 << '\n';
    std::cout << "Shared pointer 2 points at: " << *p2 << '\n';
    std::cout << "Shared pointer 3 points at: " << *p3 << '\n';
}
```

Output:

```
Shared pointer 1 points at: 123
Shared pointer 2 points at: 123
Shared pointer 3 points at: 123
```

When all pointers get out of scope, the pointed-to object gets destroyed, and the memory for it gets deallocated.

The main differences between unique and shared pointers are

- With unique pointers, we have one pointer pointing at and owning a single object, whereas with shared pointers, we have multiple pointers pointing at and owning a single object.

- Unique pointers cannot be copied, whereas shared pointers can.

If you wonder which one to use, let us say that 90% of the time, you will be using the *unique pointer*. Shared pointers can be used to represent data structures such as graphs.

Smart pointers are class templates themselves, meaning they have member functions. We will just briefly mention they can also accept custom deleters, a code that gets executed when they get out of scope.

Notice that with smart pointers, we do not need to specify the `<some_type*>`, we just need to specify the `<some_type>`.

Important!

Prefer **smart pointers** to raw pointers. With smart pointers, we do not have to worry if we properly match calls to new with calls to delete, as we do not need them. We let the smart pointer do all the heavy lifting.

CHAPTER 36

Exercises

static_cast Conversion

Write a program that uses a static_cast function to convert between fundamental types.

```cpp
#include <iostream>

int main()
{
    int x = 123;
    double d = 456.789;
    bool b = true;
    double doubleresult = static_cast<double>(x);
    std::cout << "Int to double: " << doubleresult << '\n';
    int intresult = static_cast<int>(d); // double to int
    std::cout << "Double to int: " << intresult << '\n';
    bool boolresult = static_cast<bool>(x); // int to bool
    std::cout << "Int to bool: " << boolresult << '\n';
}
```

Output:

```
Int to double: 123
Double to int: 456
Int to bool: 1
```

© Slobodan Dmitrović 2023
S. Dmitrović, *Modern C++ for Absolute Beginners*, https://doi.org/10.1007/978-1-4842-9274-7_36

A Simple Unique Pointer

Write a program that defines a unique pointer to an integer value. Use the std::make_unique function to create a pointer.

```
#include <iostream>
#include <memory>

int main()
{
    std::unique_ptr<int> p = std::make_unique<int>(123);
    std::cout << "The value of a pointed-to object is: " << *p << '\n';
}
```

Output:

```
The value of a pointed-to object is: 123
```

Unique Pointer to an Object of a Class

Write a program that defines a class with two data members, a user-defined constructor, and one member function. Create a unique pointer to an object of a class. Use the smart pointer to access the member function.

```
#include <iostream>
#include <memory>

class MyClass
{
private:
    int x;
    double d;
public:
    MyClass(int xx, double dd)
        : x{ xx }, d{ dd }
    {}
```

```
    void printdata()
    {
        std::cout << "Data members values are: " << x << " and: " << d;
    }
};

int main()
{
    std::unique_ptr<MyClass> p = std::make_unique<MyClass>(123, 456.789);
    p->printdata();
}
```

Output:

```
Data members values are: 123 and: 456.789
```

Shared Pointer Exercise

Write a program that defines three shared pointers pointing at the same object of type *int*. Create the first pointer through a *std::make_shared* function. Create the remaining pointers by copying the first pointer. Access the pointed-to object through all the pointers.

```
#include <iostream>
#include <memory>

int main()
{
    std::shared_ptr<int> p1 = std::make_shared<int>(123);
    std::shared_ptr<int> p2 = p1;
    std::shared_ptr<int> p3 = p1;
    std::cout << "Value accessed through a first pointer: " << *p1 << '\n';
    std::cout << "Value accessed through a second pointer: " << *p2
    << '\n';
    std::cout << "Value accessed through a third pointer: " << *p3 << '\n';
}
```

Output:

```
Value accessed through a first pointer: 123
Value accessed through a second pointer: 123
Value accessed through a third pointer: 123
```

Simple Polymorphism

Write a program that defines a base class with a pure virtual member function. Create a derived class that overrides a virtual function in the base class. Create a polymorphic object of a derived class through a unique pointer to a base class. Invoke the overridden member function through a unique pointer.

```cpp
#include <iostream>
#include <memory>

class BaseClass
{
public:
    virtual void dowork() = 0;
    virtual ~BaseClass() {}
};

class DerivedClass : public BaseClass
{
public:
    void dowork() override
    {
        std::cout << "Do work from a DerivedClass." << '\n';
    }
};

int main()
{
    std::unique_ptr<BaseClass> p = std::make_unique<DerivedClass>();
    p->dowork();
} // p1 goes out of scope here
```

Output:

```
Do work from a DerivedClass.
```

Here, the *override* specifier explicitly states that the *dowork()* function in the derived class overrides the virtual function in the base class.

Here, we used the unique pointer to create and automatically destroy the object and deallocate the memory once the pointer goes out of scope in the *main()* function.

Polymorphism II

Write a program that defines a base class with a pure virtual member function. Derive two classes from the base class and override the virtual function behavior. Create two unique pointers of base class type to objects of these derived classes. Use the pointers to invoke the proper polymorphic behavior.

```cpp
#include <iostream>
#include <memory>

class BaseClass
{
public:
    virtual void dowork() = 0;
    virtual ~BaseClass() {}
};

class DerivedClass : public BaseClass
{
public:
    void dowork() override
    {
        std::cout << "Do work from a DerivedClass." << '\n';
    }
};

class SecondDerivedClass : public BaseClass
{
```

```
public:
    void dowork() override
    {
        std::cout << "Do work from a SecondDerivedClass." << '\n';
    }
};

int main()
{
    std::unique_ptr<BaseClass> p = std::make_unique<DerivedClass>();
    p->dowork();
    std::unique_ptr<BaseClass> p2 = std::make_unique<SecondDerivedClass>();
    p2->dowork();
} // p1 and p2 go out of scope here
```

Output:

```
Do work from a DerivedClass.
Do work from a SecondDerivedClass.
```

Exception Handling

Write a program that throws and catches an integer exception. Handle the exception and print its value:

```
#include <iostream>

int main()
{
    try
    {
        std::cout << "Throwing an integer exception with the value of 123."
        << '\n';
        int x = 123;
        throw x;
    }
```

```
    catch (int ex)
    {
        std::cout << "An integer exception of value: " << ex << " was
        caught and handled." << '\n';
    }
}
```

Output:

```
Throwing an integer exception with the value of 123.
An integer exception of value: 123 was caught and handled.
```

Multiple Exceptions

Write a program that can throw integer and double exceptions in the same try block. Implement the exception handling blocks for both exceptions.

```
#include <iostream>

int main()
{
    try
    {
        std::cout << "Throwing an int exception..." << '\n';
        throw 123;
        std::cout << "Throwing a double exception..." << '\n';
        throw 456.789;
    }
    catch (int ex)
    {
        std::cout << "Integer exception: " << ex << " caught and handled."
        << '\n';
    }
```

```
    catch (double ex)
    {
        std::cout << "Double exception: " << ex << " caught and handled."
        << '\n';
    }
}
```

Output:

```
Throwing an int exception...
Integer exception: 123 caught and handled.
```

CHAPTER 37

Input/Output Streams

We can convert our objects to streams of bytes. We can also convert streams of bytes back to objects. The I/O stream library provides such functionality.

Streams can be *output streams* and *input streams*.

Remember the std::cout and std::cin? Those are also streams. For example, the std::cout is an output stream. It takes whatever objects we supply to it and converts them to a byte stream, which then goes to our monitor. Conversely, std::cin is an input stream. It takes the input from the keyboard and converts that input to our objects.

There are different kinds of I/O streams, and here we will explain two kinds: *file streams* and *string streams*.

File Streams

We can read from a file, and we can write to a file. The standard library offers such functionality via file streams. Those file streams are defined inside the `<fstream>` header, and they are

1. `std::ifstream` – Read from a file

2. `std::ofstream` – Write to a file

3. `std::fstream` – Read from and write to a file

The `std::fstream` can both read from and write to a file, so let us use that one. To create a `std::fstream` object, we use

```
#include <fstream>

int main()
{
    std::fstream fs{ "myfile.txt" };
}
```

© Slobodan Dmitrović 2023
S. Dmitrović, *Modern C++ for Absolute Beginners*, https://doi.org/10.1007/978-1-4842-9274-7_37

This example creates a file stream called fs and associates it with a file name myfile.txt on our disk. To read from such file, line by line, we use

```
#include <iostream>
#include <fstream>
#include <string>

int main()
{
    std::fstream fs{ "myfile.txt" };
    std::string s;
    while (fs)
    {
        std::getline(fs, s); // read each line into a string
        std::cout << s << '\n';
    }
}
```

Possible Output:

```
This is line of text no. 1.
This is line of text no. 2.
This is line of text no. 3.
```

Once associated with a file name, we use our fs file stream to read each line of text from the file and print it out on a screen. To do that, we declare a string variable s, which will hold our read line of text. Inside the while *loop*, we read a line from a file to a string. This is why the std::getline function accepts a file stream and a string as arguments. Once read, we output the text line on a screen. The while loop terminates once we reach the end of the file.

To read from a file, one character at a time, we can use the file stream's >> operator:

```
#include <iostream>
#include <fstream>

int main()
{
```

```
    std::fstream fs{ "myfile.txt" };
    char c;
    while (fs >> c)
    {
        std::cout << c;
    }
}
```

Possible Output:

```
Thisislineoftextno.1.Thisislineoftextno.2.Thisislineoftextno.3.
```

This example reads the file contents one character at a time into our char variable. By default, this skips the reading of white spaces. To rectify this, we add the std::noskipws manipulator to the preceding example:

```
#include <iostream>
#include <fstream>

int main()
{
    std::fstream fs{ "myfile.txt" };
    char c;
    while (fs >> std::noskipws >> c)
    {
        std::cout << c;
    }
}
```

Possible Output:

```
This is line of text no. 1.
This is line of text no. 2.
This is line of text no. 3.
```

To write to a file, we use the file stream's insertion << operator:

```cpp
#include <fstream>

int main()
{
    std::fstream fs{ "myoutputfile.txt", std::ios::out };
    fs << "First line of text." << '\n';
    fs << "Second line of text." << '\n';
    fs << "The third line of text." << '\n';
}
```

Possible File Output:

```
First line of text.
Second line of text.
The third line of text.
```

We associate an fs object with an output file name and provide an additional std::ios::out flag which opens a file for writing and overwrites any existing myoutputfile.txt file. Then we output our text to a file stream using the << operator.

To append text to an existing file, we include the std::ios::app flag inside the file stream constructor:

```cpp
#include <fstream>

int main()
{
    std::fstream fs{ "myoutputfile.txt", std::ios::app };
    fs << "This is appended text" << '\n';
    fs << "This is also an appended text." << '\n';
}
```

Possible File Output:

```
First line of text.
Second line of text.
The third line of text.
```

```
This is appended text
This is also an appended text.
```

We can also output strings to our file using the file stream's << operator:

```cpp
#include <iostream>
#include <fstream>
#include <string>

int main()
{
    std::fstream fs{ "myoutputfile.txt", std::ios::out };
    std::string s1 = "The first string.\n";
    std::string s2 = "The second string.\n";
    fs << s1 << s2;
}
```

Possible File Output:

```
The first string.
The second string.
```

String Streams

Similarly, there is a stream that allows us to read from and write to a string. It is defined inside the <sstream> header, and there are three different string streams:

1. std::istringstream – The stream to read from a string

2. std::ostringstream – The stream to write to a string

3. std::stringstream – The stream to both read from and write to a string

We will describe the `std::stringstream` class template as it can both read from and write to a string. To create a simple string stream, we use

```
#include <sstream>

int main()
{
    std::stringstream ss;
}
```

This example creates a simple string stream using a default constructor. To create a string stream and initialize it with a string literal, we use

```
#include <iostream>
#include <sstream>

int main()
{
    std::stringstream ss{ "Hello World." };
    std::cout << ss.str();
}
```

Output:

Hello World.

Here, we created a string stream and initialized it with a string literal in a constructor. Then we used the string stream's `.str()` member function to print the content of the stream. The `.str()` member function gets the string representation of the stream. To initialize a string stream with a string, we use

```
#include <iostream>
#include <sstream>

int main()
{
    std::stringstream ss;
    ss << "Hello World.";
    std::cout << ss.str();
}
```

Output:

```
Hello World.
```

We use the string stream's member function `.str()` to assign the string stream's content to a string variable:

```
#include <iostream>
#include <string>
#include <sstream>

int main()
{
    std::stringstream ss{ "Hello World from a string stream." };
    std::string s = ss.str();
    std::cout << s;
}
```

Output:

```
Hello World from a string stream.
```

To insert data into a string stream, we use the *formatted output operator* <<:

```
#include <iostream>
#include <string>
#include <sstream>

int main()
{
    std::string s = "Hello World.";
    std::stringstream ss{ s };
    std::cout << ss.str();
}
```

Output:

```
Hello World.
```

We can also insert values of fundamental types into a string stream using the formatted output operator <<:

```
#include <iostream>
#include <sstream>

int main()
{
    char c = 'A';
    int x = 123;
    double d = 456.78;
    std::stringstream ss;
    ss << c << x << d;
    std::cout << ss.str();
}
```

Output:

```
A123456.78
```

To make the output more readable, we can insert text between the variables:

```
#include <iostream>
#include <sstream>

int main()
{
    char c = 'A';
    int x = 123;
    double d = 456.78;
    std::stringstream ss;
    ss << "The char is: " << c << ", int is: "<< x << " and double
    is: " << d;
    std::cout << ss.str();
}
```

Output:

The char is: A, int is: 123 and double is: 456.78

To output data from a stream into an object, we use the >> operator:

```
#include <iostream>
#include <sstream>
#include <string>

int main()
{
    std::string s = "A 123 456.78";
    std::stringstream ss{ s };
    char c;
    int x;
    double d;
    ss >> c >> x >> d;
    std::cout << c << ' ' << x << ' ' << d << ' ';
}
```

Output:

A 123 456.78

This example reads data from a string stream into our variables. String streams are useful for formatted input/output and when we want to convert from built-in types to a string and from a string to built-in types.

CHAPTER 38

C++ Standard Library and Friends

The C++ language is accompanied by a library called the *C++ Standard Library*. It is a collection of containers and useful functions that we access and use in our program by including the proper header file. The containers and functions inside the C++ Standard Library are defined in the std namespace. Remember the std::string type mentioned earlier? It is also a part of the standard library. The standard library is implemented through class templates. In short, prefer using the standard library to user-provided libraries for everyday tasks.

Some functionalities explained in this chapter, such as range-based for loop and lambda expressions, are part of the language itself, not the standard library. The reason we put them here is they are mostly used in conjunction with standard library facilities.

Containers

A container is a place where we store our objects. There are different categories of containers. Here, we mention the two:

- Sequential containers

- Associative containers

Sequential containers store objects in a sequence, one next to the other in memory.

© Slobodan Dmitrović 2023
S. Dmitrović, *Modern C++ for Absolute Beginners*, https://doi.org/10.1007/978-1-4842-9274-7_38

std::vector

A vector is a container defined in the <vector> header. A vector is a sequence of contiguous elements. Of what type, we may ask? Of any *non-const* type. A vector and all other containers are implemented as class templates allowing for storage of (almost) any type. To define a vector, we use the following: std::vector<some_type>. Here's a simple example of initializing a vector of five integers:

```
#include <vector>

int main()
{
    std::vector<int> v = { 1, 2, 3, 4, 5 };
}
```

Here, we defined a vector, called v, of five integer elements, and we initialized a vector using the brace initialization. We can visualize the vector's content using the following image:

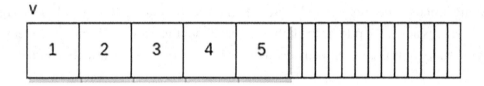

A vector can grow and shrink itself as we insert and delete elements into and from a vector. To insert an element at the end of the vector, we use the vector's .push_back() member function. Example:

```
#include <vector>

int main()
{
    std::vector<int> v = { 1, 2, 3, 4, 5 };
    v.push_back(10);
}
```

This example inserts a value of 10 at the end of our vector. We can think of the push_back function as the *insert_at_the_end* functionality:

v.push_back(10);

| 1 | 2 | 3 | 4 | 5 | 10 | | | | | | |

Now we have a container of six elements, *1 2 3 4 5 10*, and our vector in memory looks like the following:

v

| 1 | 2 | 3 | 4 | 5 | 10 | | | | | |

Vector elements are indexed. The first element has an index of 0. Individual elements can be accessed via the subscript operator [element_index] or a member function at(element_index):

```
#include <iostream>
#include <vector>

int main()
{
    std::vector<int> v = { 1, 2, 3, 4, 5 };
    std::cout << "The third element is: " << v[2] << '\n';
    std::cout << "The fourth element is :" << v.at(3) << '\n';
}
```

Output:

```
The third element is: 3
The fourth element is: 4
```

The vector's size (number of elements inside a vector) can be obtained through a .size() member function:

```
#include <iostream>
#include <vector>
```

```
int main()
{
    std::vector<int> v = { 1, 2, 3, 4, 5 };
    std::cout << "The vector's size is: " << v.size();
}
```

Output:

```
The vector's size is: 5
```

We said a vector is a sequential container. It stores elements in a sequence, one next to the other in memory. Other sequential containers are

a.   `std::list` – A doubly linked list

b.   `std::forward_list` – A singly linked list

c.   `std::deque` – A double-ended queue

So, which one to use? When in doubt, use a `std::vector`. Each of these containers has different insertions and lookup times, each serving a different purpose. Nevertheless, as far as sequence containers go, the `std::vector` is the container we want to be using most of the time.

std::array

The `std::array` is a thin wrapper around a C-style raw array. Raw arrays get converted to pointers when used as function arguments (decay to a pointer), and we should prefer the `std::array` wrapper to old C-style arrays. The `std::array` is of the following signature: `std::array<type_name, array_size>;`.

Here's a simple example:

```
#include <iostream>
#include <array>

int main()
{
    std::array<int, 5> arr = { 1, 2, 3, 4, 5 };
    for (auto el : arr)
```

```
    {
        std::cout << el << '\n';
    }
}
```

Output:

```
1
2
3
4
5
```

This example creates an array of five elements using a `std::array` container and prints them out.

Note   In modern C++, prefer `std::array` or `std::vector` to old/raw C-style arrays.

---

std::set

A set is a container that holds unique, sorted objects. It is a binary tree of sorted objects. To use a set, we must include the `<set>` header. To define a set, we use the `std::set<type>` set_name syntax. To initialize a set of five integers, we can write

```
#include <iostream>
#include <set>

int main()
{
    std::set<int> myset = { 1, 2, 3, 4, 5 };
    for (auto el : myset)
    {
        std::cout << el << '\n';
    }
}
```

Output:

1

2

3

4

5

We use the set's `.insert(value)` member function to insert an element into a set. To insert, for example, two new elements, we use

```cpp
#include <iostream>
#include <set>

int main()
{
    std::set<int> myset = { 1, 2, 3, 4, 5 };
    myset.insert(10);
    myset.insert(42);
        for (auto el : myset)
    {
        std::cout << el << '\n';
    }
}
```

Output:

1

2

3

4

5

10

42

Since the set holds unique values, the attempt to insert duplicate values will not succeed.

std::map

A map is an associative container that holds key-value pairs. Keys are sorted and unique. A map is also implemented as a balanced binary tree/graph. So now, instead of one value per element, we have two. To use a map, we need to include the header. To define a map, we use the `std::map<type1, type2> map_name` syntax. Here, `type1` represents the type of the key, and `type2` represents the type of a value. To initialize a map of `int char` pairs, for example, we can write

```
#include <map>

int main()
{
    std::map<int, char> mymap = { {1, 'a'}, {2, 'b'}, {3,'w'} };
}
```

In this example, integers are keys, and the characters are the values. Every map element is a pair. The pair's first element (the key) is accessed through a `.first` member variable, and the second element (the value) is accessed through a `.second` member variable. To print out our map, we can use

```
#include <iostream>
#include <map>

int main()
{
    std::map<int, char> mymap = { {1, 'a'}, {2, 'b'}, {3,'w'} };
    for (auto el : mymap)
    {
        std::cout << el.first << ' ' << el.second << '\n';
    }
}
```

Output:

```
1 a
2 b
3 w
```

We can also construct a map through its default constructor and some help from its key subscript operator [ ]. If the key accessed through a subscript operator does not exist, the entire key-value pair gets inserted into a map. Example:

```cpp
#include <iostream>
#include <map>

int main()
{
    std::map<int, char> mymap;
    mymap[1] = 'a';
    mymap[2] = 'b';
    mymap[3] = 'w';
    for (auto el : mymap)
    {
        std::cout << el.first << ' ' << el.second << '\n';
    }
}
```

Output:

```
1 a
2 b
3 w
```

To insert into a map, we can use the .insert() member function:

```cpp
#include <iostream>
#include <map>

int main()
{
```

```
std::map<int, char> mymap = { {1, 'a'}, {2, 'b'}, {3,'w'} };
mymap.insert({ 20, 'c' });
for (auto el : mymap)
{
    std::cout << el.first << ' ' << el.second << '\n';
}
}
```

Output:

```
1 a
2 b
3 w
20 c
```

To search for a specific key inside a map, we can use the map's `.find(key_value)` member function, which returns an iterator. If the key was not found, this function returns an iterator with a value equal to `.end()`. If the key was found, the function returns the iterator pointing at the pair containing the searched-for key:

```
#include <iostream>
#include <map>

int main()
{
    std::map<int, char> mymap = { {1, 'a'}, {2, 'b'}, {3,'w'} };
    auto it = mymap.find(2);
    if (it != mymap.end())
    {
        std::cout << "Found: " << it->first << " " << it->second << '\n';
    }
    else
    {
        std::cout << "Not found.";
    }
}
```

Output:

```
Found: 2 b
```

The iterator now points at a map element. Map elements are pairs that consist of the first element – the key – and the second element, the value. To access these using an iterator, first, we must dereference an iterator using the arrow operator ->. Then we call the pair's `first` member variable for a key and `second` for a value.

std::pair

The *std::pair* class template is a wrapper that can represent a pair of values. To use the std::pair, we need to include the *<utility>* header. To access the first value in a pair, we use the *.first* member variable. To access the second value in a pair, we use the *.second* member variable. Example:

```cpp
#include <iostream>
#include <utility>

int main()
{
    std::pair<int, double> mypair = { 123, 3.14 };
    std::cout << "The first element is: " << mypair.first << '\n';
    std::cout << "The second element is: " << mypair.second << '\n';
}
```

Output:

```
The first element is: 123
The second element is: 3.14
```

Another way to create a pair is through a *std::make_pair* function:

```cpp
#include <iostream>
#include <utility>

int main()
{
```

```
    int x = 123;
    double d = 3.14;
    std::pair<int, double> mypair = std::make_pair(x, d);
    std::cout << "The first element is: " << mypair.first << '\n';
    std::cout << "The second element is: " << mypair.second << '\n';
}
```

Output:

```
The first element is: 123
The second element is: 3.14
```

Other Containers

There are other less used containers in the standard library as well. We will mention a few of them:

    a.   `std::forward_list` – A singly linked list

    b.   `std::list` – A doubly linked list

    c.   `std::deque` – A double-ended container that allows insertion and deletion at both ends

The Range-Based for Loop

Now is an excellent time to introduce the range-based for loop, which allows us to iterate over the container/range content. The range-based for loop is of the following syntax:

```
for (some_type element_name : container_name)
{
}
```

We read it as for each `element_name` of `some_type` inside the `container_name` (do something inside the code block {}). To iterate over the elements of a vector, we can use

```cpp
#include <iostream>
#include <vector>

int main()
{
    std::vector<int> v = { 1, 2, 3, 4, 5 };
    v.push_back(10);
    for (int el : v)
    {
        std::cout << el << '\n';
    }
}
```

Output:

```
1
2
3
4
5
10
```

The el name represents *a copy of each of the vector's elements.* If we want to operate on the actual vector elements, we use a reference type:

```cpp
#include <iostream>
#include <vector>

int main()
{
    std::vector<int> v = { 1, 2, 3, 4, 5 };
    v.push_back(10);
    for (int& el : v)
    {
```

```
        std::cout << el << '\n';
    }
}
```

Output:

```
1
2
3
4
5
10
```

Now, el is *the actual vector element,* so any changes we make on el will be the changes to actual vector elements.

We can also use the auto specifier and let the compiler deduce the type of the elements in the container:

```
#include <iostream>
#include <vector>

int main()
{
    std::vector<int> v = { 1, 2, 3, 4, 5 };
    v.push_back(10);
    for (auto el : v)
    {
        std::cout << el << '\n';
    }
}
```

Output:

```
1
2
3
```

4

5

10

To iterate over a vector of strings, we would use a const auto& specifier, as we should pass strings via const reference for performance reasons:

```cpp
#include <iostream>
#include <vector>
#include <string>

int main()
{
    std::vector<std::string> v = { "Hello", "World,", "C++"};
    v.push_back("Is great!");
    for (const auto& el : v)
    {
        std::cout << el << '\n';
    }
}
```

Output:

```
Hello
World,
C++
Is great!
```

Iterators

Containers have iterators. Iterators are pointer-like entities capable of pointing to individual container elements. The iterator pointing at the first element of a vector is expressed through a .begin() member function. The iterator pointing at the (not the last but) one past the last element is expressed through a .end() member function.

For a vector of five elements, we can visualize its iterators using the following image:

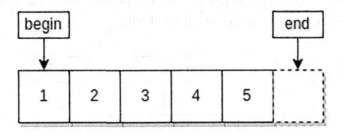

Iterators can be incremented or decremented. Let us print the vector's content using iterators:

```
#include <iostream>
#include <vector>

int main()
{
    std::vector<int> v = { 1, 2, 3, 4, 5 };
    for (auto it = v.begin(); it!=v.end(); it++)
    {
        std::cout << *it << '\n';
    }
}
```

Output:

```
1
2
3
4
5
```

As long as our vector's iterator it is not equal to v.end(), we continue iterating through a vector. When a current iterator it becomes equal to v.end(), the for loop terminates. v.end() is a signal that the end of the container (not the last element, it is one past last) has been reached. One learns to appreciate the ease of use of range-based for loops instead of this old-school iterator usage in a for loop.

Now that we know about iterators, we can use them to erase elements from a vector. Let us say we want to erase the fourth element. We position the iterator to the fourth element so that our image now looks like the following:

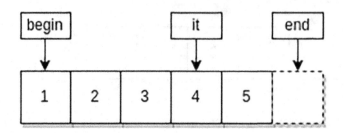

And use the .erase(iterator_name) member function:

```
#include <iostream>
#include <vector>

int main()
{
    std::vector<int> v = { 1, 2, 3, 4, 5 };
    auto it = v.begin() + 3;
    v.erase(it);
    for (auto el : v)
    {
        std::cout << el << '\n';
    }
}
```

Output:

1
2
3
5

Please note that due to the nature of the vector's implementation, it is not sufficient only to use the .erase function to remove the element from the container. Instead, we should use the so-called *erase-remove* idiom for vectors and rewrite the preceding code as follows:

```cpp
#include <iostream>
#include <vector>

int main()
{
    std::vector<int> v = { 1, 2, 3, 4, 5 };
    auto it = v.begin() + 3;
    // erase-remove idiom
    v.erase(std::remove(v.begin(), v.end(), *it), v.end());
    for (auto el : v)
    {
        std::cout << el << '\n';
    }
}
```

Output:

```
1
2
3
5
```

A call to `std::remove` is usually followed by a call to the container's `.erase` member function, thus ensuring the proper removal/deletion of the container's element.

We also mentioned another group of containers called *associative containers*. These containers are implemented as binary trees. They allow for quick search times, and the data in these containers are sorted. These associative containers are *std::set* and *std::map*. The set holds unique values. The map holds pairs of key-value elements. Maps hold unique keys. Please note that there is also another group of associative containers that allow for duplicate values. They are *std::multiset* and *std::multimap*.

Algorithms and Utilities

The C++ Standard Library provides a set of useful functions located in the `<algorithm>` header. These functions allow us to perform various operations on our containers.

std::sort

For example, if we want to sort our container, we can use the std::sort function. To sort our vector in ascending order, we use

```
#include <iostream>
#include <vector>
#include <algorithm>

int main()
{
    std::vector<int> v = { 1, 5, 2, 15, 3, 10 };
    std::sort(v.begin(), v.end());
    for (auto el : v)
    {
        std::cout << el << '\n';
    }
}
```

Output:

```
1
2
3
5
10
15
```

The std::sort function sorts a range of elements. It accepts arguments representing the start and the end of the range (one past the end of the range, to be exact). Here, we passed in the entire vector's range, where v.begin() represents the beginning and v.end() represents one past the end of the range.

To sort a container in descending order, we pass in an additional argument called a *comparator*. There is a built-in comparator called std::greater, which does the comparisons using the operator > and allows the std::sort function to sort the data in ascending order. Example:

```
#include <iostream>
#include <vector>
#include <algorithm>
#include <functional>

int main()
{
    std::vector<int> v = { 1, 5, 2, 15, 3, 10 };
    std::sort(v.begin(), v.end(), std::greater<int>());
    for (auto el : v)
    {
        std::cout << el << '\n';
    }
}
```

Output:

```
15
10
5
3
2
1
```

A comparator or a comparison function is a so-called *function object* defined inside the <functional> header. We can define our custom function object via the so-called unnamed functions called *lambda functions* or *lambdas*. More on this later in the book.

The third parameter of the std::sort function is often called a *predicate*. A predicate is a function or a function object returning true or false. Standard library functions such as the std::sort accept predicates as one of their arguments.

std::find

To find a certain element by value and return an iterator pointing at that element, we use the std::find function. To search for a value of 5 in our vector, we use

```cpp
#include <iostream>
#include <vector>
#include <algorithm>

int main()
{
    std::vector<int> v = { 1, 5, 2, 15, 3, 10 };
    auto result = std::find(v.begin(), v.end(), 5);
    if (result!=v.end())
    {
        std::cout << "Element found: " << *result;
    }
    else
    {
        std::cout << "Element not found.";
    }
}
```

Output:

```
Element found: 5
```

If the element is found, the function returns an iterator pointing at the first found element in the container. If the value is not found, the function returns a .end() iterator.

Instead of using the container's .begin() and .end() member functions, we can also use freestanding std::begin(container_name) and std::end(container_name) functions:

```cpp
#include <iostream>
#include <vector>
#include <algorithm>
#include <iterator>
```

```
int main()
{
    std::vector<int> v = { 1, 5, 2, 15, 3, 10 };
    auto result = std::find(std::begin(v), std::end(v), 5);
    if (result!=std::end(v))
    {
        std::cout << "An element found: " << *result;
    }
    else
    {
        std::cout << "Element not found.";
    }
}
```

Output:

```
An element found: 5
```

There is also a conditional `std::find_if` function which accepts a predicate. Depending on the predicate value, the function performs a search on elements for which the predicate returns `true`. More on this when we discuss *lambda expressions* in later chapters.

std::copy

The *std::copy* function copies the elements from one container to another. It can copy a range of elements marked with (*starting_position_iterator, ending_position_iterator*) from the starting container to a specific position marked with (*destination_position_iterator*) in the destination container. The function is declared inside the *<algorithm>* header. Before we copy the elements, we need to reserve enough space in the destination vector by supplying the size to a vector's constructor. Example:

```
#include <iostream>
#include <vector>
#include <algorithm>
```

```
int main()
{
    std::vector<int> copy_from_v = { 1, 2, 3, 4, 5 };
    std::vector<int> copy_to_v(5); // reserve the space for 5 elements
    std::copy(copy_from_v.begin(), copy_from_v.end(), copy_to_v.begin());
    for (auto el : copy_to_v)
    {
        std::cout << el << '\n';
    }
}
```

Output:

```
1
2
3
4
5
```

Explanation: We define a source vector called *copy_from_v* and initialize it with some values. Then we define a *copy_to_v* destination vector and reserve enough space for it to hold five elements by supplying the number 5 to its constructor. Then we copy all the elements from the beginning to the end of a source vector to the (beginning of) destination vector.

To copy only the first three elements, we would use the appropriate range marked with *copy_from_v.begin()* and *copy_from_v.begin() + 3*. And we only need to reserve the space for three elements in the destination vector:

```
#include <iostream>
#include <vector>
#include <algorithm>

int main()
{
    std::vector<int> copy_from_v = { 1, 2, 3, 4, 5 };
    std::vector<int> copy_to_v(3);
```

```
std::copy(copy_from_v.begin(), copy_from_v.begin() + 3, copy_to_v.
begin());
for (auto el : copy_to_v)
{
    std::cout << el << '\n';
}
}
```

Output:

```
1
2
3
```

Min and Max Elements

To find the greatest element in the container, we use the *std::max_element* function declared in the <algorithm> header. This function returns an iterator to the max element in the container:

```
#include <iostream>
#include <vector>
#include <algorithm>

int main()
{
    std::vector<int> v = { 1, 2, 3, 4, 5 };
    auto it = std::max_element(std::begin(v), std::end(v));
    std::cout << "The max element in the vector is: " << *it;
}
```

Output:

```
The max element in the vector is: 5
```

Similarly, to find the smallest element in the container, we use the *std::min_element* function, which returns an iterator to the min element in the container or a range:

```cpp
#include <iostream>
#include <vector>
#include <algorithm>

int main()
{
    std::vector<int> v = { 1, 2, 3, 4, 5 };
    auto it = std::min_element(std::begin(v), std::end(v));
    std::cout << "The min element in the vector is: " << *it;
}
```

   Output:

```
The min element in the vector is: 1
```

Lambda Expressions

Lambda expressions, or lambdas for short, are the so-called *anonymous function objects*. A function object, or a *functor*, is an object of a class that can be called as a function. To be able to call an object like a function, we must overload the *function call operator ()* for our class:

```cpp
#include <iostream>

class MyClass
{
public:
    void operator()()
    {
        std::cout << "Function object called." << '\n';
    }
};
```

```
int main()
{
    MyClass myobject;
    myobject(); // invoke the function object
}
```

Output:

```
Function object called.
```

The function object can have one or more parameters; in this case, there is one parameter called x:

```
#include <iostream>

class MyClass
{
public:
    void operator()(int x)
    {
        std::cout << "Function object with a parameter " << x << "
        called.";
    }
};

int main()
{
    MyClass myobject;
    myobject(123); // invoke the function object
}
```

Output:

```
Function object with a parameter 123 called.
```

The function object can also return a value. For example, the following function object checks if the parameter is an even number:

```cpp
#include <iostream>

class MyClass
{
public:
    bool operator()(int x)
    {
        if (x % 2 == 0)
        {
            return true;
        }
        else
        {
            return false;
        }
    }
};

int main()
{
    MyClass myobject;
    bool isEven = myobject(123);
    if (isEven)
    {
        std::cout << "The number is even." << '\n';
    }
    else
    {
        std::cout << "The number is odd." << '\n';
    }
}
```

Output:

```
The number is odd.
```

It is said that function objects carry their values. Since they are objects of a class, they can have data members they carry with them. This separates them from regular functions.

As we can see, overloading the operator ( ) and writing the entire class can be cumbersome if we only want a simple function object. That is where the lambda expressions come into play. Lambda expressions are anonymous/unnamed function objects. The lambda expression signature is

```
[captures](parameters){lambda_body};
```

To define and invoke a simple lambda, we use

```
#include <iostream>

int main()
{
    auto mylambda = []() {std::cout << "Hello from a lambda
    expression."; };
    mylambda();
}
```

Output:

```
Hello from a lambda expression.
```

Here, we assign the result of a lambda expression []() {std::cout << "Hello from a lambda expression."; } to a variable mylambda. Then we invoke this lambda by using the function call operator (). Since lambdas are unnamed functions, here we gave it the name of mylambda, to be able to invoke the code from the lambda expression itself.

To be able to use the variables in the scope in which the lambda was defined, we need to *capture* them first. The capture section marked by [ ] can *capture* local variables by copy:

```
#include <iostream>

int main()
{
    int x = 123;
    auto mylambda = [x]() { std::cout << "The value of x is: " << x; };
    mylambda();
}
```

Output:

```
The value of x is: 123
```

Here, we captured the local variable x by value and used it inside our lambda body. Another way to capture variables is by reference, where we use the [&name] notation. Example:

```
#include <iostream>

int main()
{
    int x = 123;
    auto mylambda = [&x]() {
        x++;
        std::cout << "The value of x is: " << x;
    };
    mylambda();
}
```

Output:

```
The value of x is: 124
```

To capture more than one variable, we use the comma operator in the capture list: [var1, var2]. For example, to capture two local variables by value, we use

```cpp
#include <iostream>

int main()
{
    int x = 123;
    int y = 456;
    auto mylambda = [x, y]() { std::cout << "The x is: " << x << ", and y
    is: " << y; };
    mylambda();
}
```

   Output:

```
The x is: 123, and y is: 456
```

To capture both local variables by reference, we use

```cpp
#include <iostream>

int main()
{
    int x = 123;
    int y = 456;
    auto mylambda = [&x, &y]() {
        x++;
        y++;
        std::cout << "The x is: " << x << ", and y is: " << y;
    };
    mylambda();
}
```

   Output:

```
The x is: 124, and y is: 457
```

Lambdas can have optional parameters inside the parentheses: [](param1, param2) {}. Example:

```
#include <iostream>

int main()
{
    auto mylambda = [](int x, int y)
    {
        std::cout << "The value of x is: " << x << ", and y is: " << y;
    };
    mylambda(123, 456);
}
```

Output:

```
The value of x is: 123, and y is: 456
```

Lambdas are most often used as predicates inside the standard library algorithm functions. For example, if we want to count the number of even elements in the container, we would supply a lambda to a std::count_if function. Example:

```
#include <iostream>
#include <vector>
#include <algorithm>

int main()
{
    std::vector<int> v = { 1, 2, 3, 4, 5, 6, 7, 8, 9, 10, 20, 30 };
    auto counteven = std::count_if(std::begin(v), std::end(v),
        [](int x) {return x % 2 == 0; });
    std::cout << "The number of even vector elements is: " << counteven;
}
```

Output:

```
The number of even vector elements is: 7
```

Here, we have a lambda function that checks if an argument is an even number and returns true if it is. This lambda is then used as a predicate inside the std::count_if function. This function only counts the numbers for which the predicate (our lambda expression) returns true. The std::count_if function iterates through all the vector elements, and each element becomes a lambda argument.

We can use lambdas in other standard library algorithm functions accepting expressions named *callables*. Examples of callables are lambdas and function objects.

By using lambdas, we can more clearly express ourselves, and we do not have to write the verbose class function objects. Lambdas were introduced in the C++11 standard.

CHAPTER 39

Exercises

Basic Vector

Write a program that defines a vector of integers. Insert two elements into a vector. Print out the vector content using the range-based for loop.

```cpp
#include <iostream>
#include <vector>

int main()
{
    std::vector<int> v = { 10, 5, 8, 4, 1, 2 };
    v.push_back(15); // insert the value 15
    v.push_back(30); // insert the value of 30
    for (auto el : v)
    {
        std::cout << el << '\n';
    }
}
```

Output:

```
10
5
8
4
1
```

© Slobodan Dmitrović 2023
S. Dmitrović, *Modern C++ for Absolute Beginners*, https://doi.org/10.1007/978-1-4842-9274-7_39

2

15

30

Deleting a Single Value

Write a program that defines a vector of integers. Erase the second element from the vector. Print out the vector content using the range-based loop.

```cpp
#include <iostream>
#include <vector>

int main()
{
    std::vector<int> v = { 10, 5, 8, 4, 1, 2 };
    v.erase(v.begin() + 1); // erase the second element which is 5
    for (auto el : v)
    {
        std::cout << el << '\n';
    }
}
```

Output:

10

8

4

1

2

Deleting a Range of Elements

Write a program that defines a vector of integers. Erase the range of three elements starting from the beginning of the vector. Print out the vector content using the range-based for loop.

```
#include <iostream>
#include <vector>

int main()
{
    std::vector<int> v = { 10, 5, 8, 4, 1, 2 };
    v.erase(v.begin(), v.begin() + 3); // erase the first 3 elements
    for (auto el : v)
    {
        std::cout << el << '\n';
    }
}
```

Output:

```
4
1
2
```

In this case, the .erase() function overload accepts two arguments. One is the beginning of the range to be deleted. In our case, it is marked with v.begin(). The second argument is the end of the range to be deleted. In our case, it is the v.begin() + 3 iterator. Please note that instead of the .begin() member function, we could have used a freestanding std::begin(v) function.

Finding Elements in a Vector

Write a program that searches for a vector element using the std::find() algorithm function. If the element has been found, delete it. Print out the vector content.

```
#include <iostream>
#include <vector>
#include <algorithm>
```

```cpp
int main()
{
    std::vector<int> v = { 10, 5, 8, 4, 1, 2 };
    int findnumber = 4;
    auto foundit = std::find(std::begin(v), std::end(v), findnumber);
    if (foundit != std::end(v))
    {
        std::cout << "Element found. Deleting the element." << '\n';
        v.erase(foundit);
        std::cout << "Element deleted." << '\n';
    }
    else
    {
        std::cout << "Element not found." << '\n';
    }
    for (auto el : v)
    {
        std::cout << el << '\n';
    }
}
```

Output:

```
Element found. Deleting the element.
Element deleted.
10
5
8
1
2
```

Basic Set

Write a program that defines a set of integers. Print out the set content and observe the following: the data is sorted, regardless of how we define the set. This is because, internally, std::set is a sorted container that holds unique values.

```
#include <iostream>
#include <set>

int main()
{
    std::set<int> myset = { -10, 1, 3, 5, -20, 6, 9, 15 };
    for (auto el : myset)
    {
        std::cout << el << '\n';
    }
}
```

   Output:

```
-20
-10
1
3
5
6
9
15
```

Set Data Manipulation

Write a program that defines a set and inserts two new values using the set's .insert() member function. Then, delete one arbitrary value from a set using the set's .erase() member function. Print out the set content afterward.

```
#include <iostream>
#include <set>

int main()
{
    std::set<int> myset = { -10, 1, 3, 5, 6, 9, 15 };
    myset.insert(-5); // inserts a value of -5
    myset.insert(30); // inserts a value of 30
```

```
    myset.erase(6); // deletes a value of 6
    for (auto el : myset)
    {
        std::cout << el << '\n';
    }
}
```

Output:

```
-10
-5
1
3
5
9
15
30
```

Set Member Functions

Write a program that defines a set of integers and utilizes the set's member function to check the set's size, check whether it is empty, and clear the set's content.

```
#include <iostream>
#include <set>

int main()
{
    std::set<int> myset = { -10, 1, 3, 5, 6, 9, 15 };
    std::cout << "The set's size is: " << myset.size() << '\n';
    std::cout << "Clearing the set..." << '\n';
    myset.clear(); // clear the set's content
    if (myset.empty())
    {
        std::cout << "The set is empty." << '\n';
    }
```

```
    else
    {
        std::cout << "The set is not empty." << '\n';
    }
}
```

Output:

```
The set's size is: 7
Clearing the set...
The set is empty.
```

Search for Data in a Set

Write a program that searches for a particular value in a set using the set's .find()
member function. If the value is found, delete it. Print out the set content.

```cpp
#include <iostream>
#include <set>

int main()
{
    std::set<int> myset = { -10, 1, 3, 5, 6, 9, 15 };
    int findvalue = 5;
    auto foundit = myset.find(findvalue);
    if (foundit != myset.end())
    {
        std::cout << "Value found. Deleting the value..." << '\n';
        myset.erase(foundit);
        std::cout << "Element deleted." << '\n';
    }
    else
    {
        std::cout << "Value not found." << '\n';
    }
```

```
    for (auto el : myset)
    {
        std::cout << el << '\n';
    }
}
```

Output:

```
Value found. Deleting the value...
Element deleted.
-10
1
3
6
9
15
```

Basic Map

Write a program that defines a map where keys are of type char and values are of type int. Print out the map's content.

```
#include <iostream>
#include <map>

int main()
{
    std::map<char, int> mymap = { {'a', 1}, {'b', 5}, {'e', 10},
    {'f', 10} };
    for (auto el : mymap)
    {
        std::cout << el.first << ' ' << el.second << '\n';
    }
}
```

Output:

```
a 1
b 5
e 10
f 10
```

Explanation:

Map elements are key-value pairs. These pairs are represented by a *std::pair* class template which can store a pair. So the type of a map element is *std::pair<char, int>*. In a map container, keys are unique, and values do not have to be unique. We initialize the map with our key-value pairs inside the initializer list {}. Using a range-based for loop, we iterate over map elements. To access the key in a pair, we use the pair's *.first* member function, which represents the first element in a pair – in our case, the key. Similarly, we access the second element using the pair's *.second* member function, which represents the map element value.

Inserting into a Map

Write a program that defines a map of strings and integers. Insert an element into a map using the map's .insert() member function. Then use the map's operator [ ] to insert another key-value element into a map. Print the map's content afterward.

```cpp
#include <iostream>
#include <map>
#include <string>

int main()
{
    std::map<std::string, int> mymap = { {"red", 1}, {"green", 20},
    {"blue", 15} };
    mymap.insert({ "magenta", 4 });
    mymap["yellow"] = 5;
```

```
    for (const auto& el : mymap)
    {
        std::cout << el.first << ' ' << el.second << '\n';
    }
}
```

Output:

```
blue 15
green 20
magenta 4
red 1
yellow 5
```

When using the map's [ ] operator, there are two scenarios. The key inside the [ ] operator exists in the map. This means we can use it to change the value of an element. The key does not exist. In this case, when using the map's operator [], the key-value element gets inserted into the map. This was the case with our mymap["yellow"] = 5; statement. Remember, maps are graphs, and the map's elements are sorted based on a key. And since our keys are strings, the order does not necessarily need to be the one we provided in the initializer list.

If, for example, we have a map of ints and strings, and we provide sorted int keys in the initializer list, the order would be the same when printing out the elements:

```
#include <iostream>
#include <map>
#include <string>

int main()
{
    std::map<int, std::string> mymap = { {1, "First"}, {2, "Second"}, {3,
    "Third"}, {4, "Fourth"} };
    for (const auto& el : mymap)
    {
        std::cout << el.first << ' ' << el.second << '\n';
    }
}
```

Output:

```
1 First
2 Second
3 Third
4 Fourth
```

Searching and Deleting from a Map

Write a program that defines a map of integers and strings. Search for an element by key using the map's *.find()* member function. If the element is found, delete it. Print out the map content.

```cpp
#include <iostream>
#include <map>
#include <string>

int main()
{
    std::map<int, std::string> mymap = { {1, "First"}, {2, "Second"}, {3,
    "Third"}, {4, "Fourth"} };
    int findbykey = 2;
    auto foundit = mymap.find(findbykey);
    if (foundit != mymap.end())
    {
        std::cout << "Key found." << '\n';
        std::cout << "Deleting the element..." << '\n';
        mymap.erase(foundit);
    }
    else
    {
        std::cout << "Key not found." << '\n';
    }
```

```
    for (const auto& el : mymap)
    {
        std::cout << el.first << ' ' << el.second << '\n';
    }
}
```

Output:

```
Key found.
Deleting the element...
1 First
3 Third
4 Fourth
```

Lambda Expressions

Write a program that defines a vector of integers. Sort the vector in a descending order using the *std::sort* function and a user-provided lambda function as a predicate.

```
#include <iostream>
#include <vector>
#include <algorithm>

int main()
{
    std::vector<int> v = { 5, 10, 4, 1, 3, 15 };
    std::sort(std::begin(v), std::end(v), [](int x, int y) {return x
    > y; });
    for (const auto& el : v)
    {
        std::cout << el << '\n';
    }
}
```

Output:

```
15
10
5
4
3
1
```

Write a program that defines a vector of integers. Use the *std::count_if* function and a user-provided lambda function to count only even numbers.

```
#include <iostream>
#include <vector>
#include <algorithm>

int main()
{
    std::vector<int> v = { 5, 10, 4, 1, 3, 8 };
    int mycount = std::count_if(std::begin(v), std::end(v), [](int x)
    {return x % 2 == 0; });
    std::cout << "The number of even numbers is: " << mycount;
}
```

Output:

```
The number of even numbers is: 3
```

Now, let us write a program that defines a local lambda expression that can capture and modify the variable defined inside the main() function:

```
#include <iostream>

int main()
{
    int x = 123;
    std::cout << "The value of a local variable is: " << x << '\n';
    auto mylambda = [&x](){ x++; };
```

```
    mylambda();
    std::cout << "Lambda captured and changed the local variable to: "
    << x << '\n';
}
```

Output:

```
The value of a local variable is: 123
Lambda captured and changed the local variable to: 124
```

CHAPTER 40

C++ Standards

C++ is an ISO standardized programming language. There are different C++ standards: *C++98, C++03, C++11, C++14, C++17, C++20,* and *C++23.*

Everything starting with C++11 is referred to as "modern C++." These standards define the language in great technical detail. They also serve as manuals for C++ compiler writers. It is a mind-boggling set of rules and specifications. The C++ standards can be bought, or a draft version can be downloaded for free. These drafts closely resemble the final C++ standard. When C++ code can be successfully transferred and compiled on different platforms (machines or compilers), and when C++ implementation closely follows the standard, we say that the code is *portable.* This is often referred to as *portable C++.*

The standards surrounded by braces represent the so-called "modern C++." Each standard describes the language and introduces new language and library features. It may also introduce changes to the existing rules. We will describe notable features in each of these standards.

C++11

C++11 is an ISO C++ standard published in 2011. To compile for this standard, add the *-std=c++11* flag to a command-line compilation string if compiling with g++ or clang. If using Visual Studio, choose *Project* ➤ *Options* ➤ *Configuration Properties* ➤ *C/C++* ➤ *Language* ➤ *C++ Language Standard* and choose *C++11.* New Visual Studio versions already support this standard out of the box. We have already described the notable C++11 features in previous chapters, and here we will briefly go through them once again and introduce a few new ones.

© Slobodan Dmitrović 2023
S. Dmitrović, *Modern C++ for Absolute Beginners*, https://doi.org/10.1007/978-1-4842-9274-7_40

Automatic Type Deduction

This standard introduces the auto keyword, which deduces the type of the variable based on the variable's initializer:

```
int main()
{
    auto mychar = 'A';
    auto myint = 123 + 456;
    auto mydouble = 456.789;
}
```

Range-Based Loops

The range-based loops allow us to iterate over the range, such as C++ Standard Library containers:

```
#include <iostream>
#include <vector>

int main()
{
    std::vector<int> v = { 10, 20, 40, 5, -20, 75 };
    for (auto el : v)
    {
        std::cout << el << '\n';
    }
}
```

Output:

```
10
20
40
5
-20
75
```

The range-based for loop is of the following form: `for (type element : container)`. This is read as *for each element in a container* (do something).

Initializer Lists

Initializer lists, represented by braces { }, allow us to initialize objects in a *uniform way*. We can initialize single objects:

```
int main()
{
    int x{ 123 };
    int y = { 456 };
    double d{ 3.14 };
}
```

and containers:

```
#include <vector>

int main()
{
    std::vector<int> v = { 1, 2, 3, 4, 5 };
}
```

List initialization also prevents narrowing conversions. If we tried to initialize our integer object with a double value inside the initializer list, the compilation would fail:

```
int main()
{
    int x = { 123.45 }; // Error, does not allowing narrowing
}
```

When initializing our objects, we should prefer initializer lists {} to old-style parentheses ().

Move Semantics

The C++11 standard introduces the move semantics for classes. We can initialize our objects by moving the data from other objects. This is achieved through move constructors and move assignment operators. Both accept the so-called *rvalue reference* as an argument. *Lvalue* is an expression that can be used on the left-hand side of the assignment operation. *Rvalues* are expressions that can be used on the right-hand side of an assignment. The rvalue reference has the signature of *some_type&&*. To cast an expression to an rvalue reference, we use the *std::move* function. A simple move constructor and move assignment signature are

```cpp
class MyClass
{
public:
    MyClass(MyClass&& otherobject) // move constructor
    {
        //implement the move logic here
    }

    MyClass& operator=(MyClass&& otherobject) // move assignment operator
    {
        // implement the move logic here
        return *this;
    }
};
```

Lambda Expressions

Lambda expressions are anonymous function objects. They allow us to write a short code snippet to be used as a standard library function predicate. Lambdas have a capture list marked by [ ] where we can capture local variables by reference or copy, a parameter list with optional parameters marked with ( ), and a lambda body marked with { }. An empty lambda looks like [](){};. A simple example of counting only the even numbers in a set using the lambda as a predicate:

```
#include <iostream>
#include <vector>
#include <algorithm>

int main()
{
    std::vector<int> v = { 1, 2, 3, 4, 5 };
    auto counteven = std::count_if(std::begin(v), std::end(v),
        [](int x) {return x % 2 == 0; }); // lambda expression
    std::cout << "The number of even vector elements is: " << counteven;
}
```

Output:

```
The number of even vector elements is: 2
```

The constexpr Specifier

The constexpr specifier promises the variable or a function can be evaluated during compile time. If the expression cannot be evaluated during compile time, the compiler emits an error:

```
int main()
{
    constexpr int n = 123;          //OK, 123 is a compile-time constant
    // expression
    constexpr double d = 456.78;    //OK, 456.78 is a compile-time constant
    // expression
    constexpr double d2 = d;        //OK, d is a constant expression
    int x = 123;
    constexpr int n2 = x;           //compile-time error
                                    // the value of x is not known during
                                    // compile-time
}
```

285

Scoped Enumerators

The C++11 standard introduces the scoped enumerators. Unlike the old enumerators, the scoped enumerators do not *leak* their names into the surrounding scope. Scoped enums have the following signature: *enum class Enumerator_Name {value1, value2, etc.}* signature. A simple example of a scoped enum is

```cpp
enum class MyEnum
{
    myfirstvalue,
    mysecondvalue,
    mythirdvalue
};

int main()
{
    MyEnum myenum = MyEnum::myfirstvalue;
}
```

Smart Pointers

Smart pointers point to objects, and when the pointer goes out of scope, the object gets destroyed. This makes them *smart* in the sense that we do not have to worry about the manual deallocation of allocated memory. The smart pointers do all the heavy lifting for us.

There are two kinds of smart pointers, the unique pointer with a *std::unique_ptr< Type>* signature and a shared pointer with a *std::shared_ptr< Type>* signature. The difference between the two is that we can have only one unique pointer pointing at the object. In contrast, we can have multiple shared pointers pointing at an object. When the unique pointer goes out of scope, the object gets destroyed, and the memory is deallocated. When the last of the shared pointers pointing at our object goes out of scope, the object gets destroyed. The memory gets deallocated.

Here's a unique pointer example:

```cpp
#include <iostream>
#include <memory>

int main()
```

```
{
    std::unique_ptr<int> p(new int{ 123 });
    std::cout << "The pointed-to element is: " << *p;
} // p goes out of scope here, the memory gets deallocated, the object gets
  // destroyed
```

Output:

```
The pointed-to element is: 123
```

A unique pointer cannot be copied, only moved. To have multiple shared pointers pointing at the same object, we would write

```
#include <iostream>
#include <memory>

int main()
{
    std::shared_ptr<int> p1(new int{ 123 });
    std::shared_ptr<int> p2 = p1;
    std::shared_ptr<int> p3 = p1;
    std::cout << "The pointed-to element is: " << *p2;
} // when the last shared pointer goes out of scope, the memory gets
  // deallocated
```

Output:

```
The pointed-to element is: 123
```

Shared pointers can be copied. It is said they *share ownership* of the object. When the last shared pointer gets out of scope, the pointed-to object gets destroyed, and the memory gets deallocated.

std::unordered_set

The std::unordered_set is a container that allows for constant time insertion, searching, and removal of elements. This container is implemented as an array of buckets of linked lists. The hash value of each element is calculated, and the object is placed into an appropriate bucket based on the hash value. The object themselves are not sorted in any particular order. To define an unordered set, we need to include the <unordered_set> header. Example:

```
#include <iostream>
#include <unordered_set>

int main()
{
    std::unordered_set<int> myunorderedset = { 1, 2, 5, -4, 7, 10 };
    for (auto el : myunorderedset)
    {
        std::cout << el << '\n';
    }
}
```

Output:

```
1
10
2
5
7
-4
```

The values are not sorted but are unique. To insert single or multiple values into an unordered_set, we use the .insert() member function:

```
#include <iostream>
#include <unordered_set>

int main()
{
```

```
std::unordered_set<int> myunorderedset = { 1, 2, 5, -4, 7, 10 };
myunorderedset.insert(6); // insert a single value
myunorderedset.insert({ 8, 15, 20 }); // insert multiple values
for (auto el : myunorderedset)
{
    std::cout << el << '\n';
}
}
```

Output:

```
1
10
2
5
7
-4
6
8
15
20
```

To delete a value from an unordered set, we use the `.erase()` member function:

```
#include <iostream>
#include <unordered_set>

int main()
{
    std::unordered_set<int> myunorderedset = { 1, 2, 5, -4, 7, 10 };
    myunorderedset.erase(-4); // erase a single value
    for (auto el : myunorderedset)
    {
        std::cout << el << '\n';
    }
}
```

Output:

```
1
10
2
5
7
```

std::unordered_map

Similar to std::unordered_set, there is also a std::unordered_map, an unordered container of key-value pairs with unique keys. This container also allows for fast insertion, searching, and removal of elements. The container's data is implemented through buckets. What element goes into what bucket depends on the element's key hash value. To define an unordered map, we include the <unordered_map> header. Example:

```cpp
#include <iostream>
#include <unordered_map>

int main()
{
    std::unordered_map<char, int> myunorderedmap = { {'a', 1}, {'b', 2},
    {'c', 5} };
    for (auto el : myunorderedmap)
    {
        std::cout << el.first << ' '<< el.second << '\n';
    }
}
```

Output:

```
a 1
b 2
c 5
```

Here, we initialize an unordered map with key-value pairs. In the range-based for loop, we print both the key and the value. Map elements are pairs. Pairs have data members *.first* for accessing a key and *.second* for accessing a value. To insert an element into a map, we can use the `.insert()` member function:

```
#include <iostream>
#include <unordered_map>

int main()
{
    std::unordered_map<char, int> myunorderedmap = { {'a', 1}, {'b', 2},
    {'c', 5} };
    myunorderedmap.insert({ 'd', 10 });
    for (auto el : myunorderedmap)
    {
        std::cout << el.first << ' '<< el.second << '\n';
    }
}
```

Output:

```
a 1
b 2
c 5
d 10
```

We can also use the map's operator [] to insert an element. Normally, this operator is used to access an element value by key. However, if the key does not exist, the operator inserts a new element into the map:

```
#include <iostream>
#include <unordered_map>

int main()
{
    std::unordered_map<char, int> myunorderedmap = { {'a', 1}, {'b', 2},
    {'c', 5} };
    myunorderedmap['b'] = 4; // key exists, change the value
```

```
myunorderedmap['d'] = 10; // key does not exist, insert the new element
for (auto el : myunorderedmap)
{
    std::cout << el.first << ' ' << el.second << '\n';
}
}
```

Output:

```
a 1
b 4
c 5
d 10
```

std::tuple

While *std::pair* can hold only two values, the *std::tuple* wrapper can hold more than two values. To use tuples, we need to include the *<tuple>* header. To access a certain tuple element, we use the *std::get<index_of_an_element>(tuple_name)* function:

```
#include <iostream>
#include <utility>
#include <tuple>

int main()
{
    std::tuple<char, int, double> mytuple = { 'a', 123, 3.14 };
    std::cout << "The first element is: " << std::get<0>(mytuple) << '\n';
    std::cout << "The second element is: " << std::get<1>(mytuple) << '\n';
    std::cout << "The third element is: " << std::get<2>(mytuple) << '\n';
}
```

Output:

```
The first element is: a
The second element is: 123
The third element is: 3.14
```

We can create a tuple using the *std::make_tuple* function:

```
#include <iostream>
#include <tuple>
#include <string>

int main()
{
    auto mytuple = std::make_tuple<int, double, std::string>(123, 3.14,
    "Hello World.");
    std::cout << "The first tuple element is: " << std::get<0>(mytuple)
    << '\n';
    std::cout << "The second tuple element is: " << std::get<1>(mytuple)
    << '\n';
    std::cout << "The third tuple element is: " << std::get<2>(mytuple)
    << '\n';
}
```

Output:

```
The first tuple element is: 123
The second tuple element is: 3.14
The third tuple element is: Hello World.
```

Instead of typing a lengthy tuple type, which is *std::tuple<int, double, std::string>*, we used the *auto* specifier to deduce the type name for us.

static_assert

The *static_assert* directive checks a static (constexpr) condition during compile time. If the condition is false, the directive fails the compilation and displays an error message. Example:

```
int main()
{
    constexpr int x = 123;
    static_assert(x == 456, "The constexpr value is not 456.");
}
```

Here, the static_assert checks if the value of x is equal to 456 during compile time. Since it is not, the compilation will fail with a `"The constexpr value is not 456."` message. We can think of the static_assert as a way of testing our code during compile time. It is also a neat way of testing if the value of a constexpr expression is what we expect it to be.

Introduction to Concurrency

The C++11 standard introduces facilities for working with threads. To enable threading, we need to add the *-pthread* flag when compiling with g++ and clang on the command line. Example:

```
g++ -std=c++11 -Wall -pthread source.cpp
```

With clang, it will be

```
clang++ -std=c++11 -Wall -pthread source.cpp
```

When we compile and link our source code program, an executable file is produced. When we start the executable, the program gets loaded into memory and starts running. This running program is called a *process*. When we start multiple executable files, we can have multiple processes. Each process has its own memory and its own address space. Within a process, there can be multiple threads. What are threads or threads of execution? They are an OS mechanism that allows us to execute multiple pieces of code concurrently/simultaneously.

For example, we can execute multiple functions concurrently using threads. In a broader sense, concurrently can also mean *in parallel*. A thread is part of the process. A process can spawn one or more threads. Threads share the same memory and thus can communicate with each other using this shared memory.

To create a thread object, we use the *std::thread* class template from a *<thread>* header file. Once defined, the thread starts executing. To create a thread that executes a code inside a function, we supply the function name to the thread constructor as a parameter. Example:

```
#include <iostream>
#include <thread>

void function1()
```

```
{
    for (int i = 0; i < 5; i++)
    {
        std::cout << "Executing function1." << '\n';
    }
}

int main()
{
    std::thread t1{ function1 }; // create and start a thread
    t1.join(); // wait for the t1 thread to finish
}
```

Output:

```
Executing function1.
Executing function1.
Executing function1.
Executing function1.
Executing function1.
```

Here, we have defined a thread called *t1* that executes a function *function1*. We supply the function name to the std::thread constructor as a first parameter. In a way, our program now has a main thread, which is the *main()* function itself, and the t1 thread, which was created from the main thread. The *.join()* member function says: "*main thread, please wait for me to finish my work before continuing with yours.*" If we left out the *.join()* function, the main thread would finish executing before the t1 thread has finished its work. We avoid this by *joining* the child thread to the main thread.

If our function accepts parameters, we can pass those parameters when constructing the std::thread object:

```
#include <iostream>
#include <thread>
#include <string>

void function1(const std::string& param)
{
```

```cpp
    for (int i = 0; i < 5; i++)
    {
        std::cout << "Executing function1, " << param << '\n';
    }
}

int main()
{
    std::thread t1{ function1, "Hello World from a thread." };
    t1.join();
}
```

Output:

```
Executing function1, Hello World from a thread.
Executing function1, Hello World from a thread.
Executing function1, Hello World from a thread.
Executing function1, Hello World from a thread.
Executing function1, Hello World from a thread.
```

We can spawn multiple threads in our program/process by constructing multiple std::thread objects. Here's an example where we have two threads executing two different functions concurrently/in parallel:

```cpp
#include <iostream>
#include <thread>

void function1()
{
    for (int i = 0; i < 5; i++)
    {
        std::cout << "Executing function1." << '\n';
    }
}

void function2()
{
    for (int i = 0; i < 5; i++)
```

```
    {
        std::cout << "Executing function2." << '\n';
    }
}

int main()
{
    std::thread t1{ function1 };
    std::thread t2{ function2 };
    t1.join();
    t2.join();
}
```

Possible Output:

```
Executing function1.
Executing function1.
Executing function1.
Executing function1.
Executing function1.
Executing function2.
Executing function2.
Executing function2.
Executing function2.
Executing function2.
```

This example creates two threads executing two different functions concurrently.

The *function1* code executes in a thread *t1*, and the *function2* code executes in a separate thread called *t2*.

We can also have multiple threads executing code from the same function concurrently:

```
#include <iostream>
#include <thread>
#include <string>

void myfunction(const std::string& param)
{
```

```
    for (int i = 0; i < 5; i++)
    {
        std::cout << "Executing function from a " << param << '\n';
    }
}

int main()
{
    std::thread t1{ myfunction, "Thread 1" };
    std::thread t2{ myfunction, "Thread 2" };
    t1.join();
    t2.join();
}
```

Possible Output:

```
Executing function from a Thread 2
Executing function from a Thread 2
Executing function from a Thread 2
Executing function from a Thread 2
Executing function from a Thread 1
Executing function from a Thread 1
Executing function from a Thread 1
Executing function from a Thread 1
Executing function from a Thread 1
Executing function from a Thread 2
```

Threads sometimes need to access the same object. In our example, both threads are accessing the global *std::cout* object in order to output the data. This can be a problem. Accessing the *std::cout* object from two different threads at the same time allows one thread to write a little to it, then another thread jumps in and writes a little to it, and we can end up with some strange text in the console window:

Executi.Executingng function1.Executing function2.

This means we need to synchronize the access to a shared *std::cout* object somehow. While one thread is writing to it, we need to ensure that the thread does not write to it.

We do so by locking and unlocking mutexes. A mutex is represented by a *std::mutex* class template from a *<mutex>* header. A mutex is a way to synchronize access to shared objects between multiple threads. A thread owns a mutex once it locks the mutex, then performs access to shared data and unlocks the mutex when access to shared data is no longer needed. This ensures only one thread at a time can have access to a shared object, which is *std::cout* in our case.

Here is an example where two threads execute the same function and guard access to the std::cout object by locking and unlocking mutexes:

```cpp
#include <iostream>
#include <thread>
#include <string>
#include <mutex>

std::mutex m; // will guard std::cout

void myfunction(const std::string& param)
{
    for (int i = 0; i < 5; i++)
    {
        m.lock();
        std::cout << "Executing function from a " << param << '\n';
        m.unlock();
    }
}

int main()
{
    std::thread t1{ myfunction, "Thread 1" };
    std::thread t2{ myfunction, "Thread 2" };
    t1.join();
    t2.join();
}
```

Possible Output:

```
Executing function from a Thread 1
Executing function from a Thread 1
Executing function from a Thread 1
Executing function from a Thread 1
Executing function from a Thread 1
Executing function from a Thread 2
Executing function from a Thread 2
Executing function from a Thread 2
Executing function from a Thread 2
Executing function from a Thread 2
```

Since we can forget to unlock the mutex manually, a better approach is to use the *std::lock_guard* function instead. It locks the mutex, and once it goes out of scope, it automatically unlocks the mutex. Example:

```cpp
#include <iostream>
#include <thread>
#include <string>
#include <mutex>

std::mutex m; // will guard std::cout

void myfunction(const std::string& param)
{
    for (int i = 0; i < 5; i++)
    {
        std::lock_guard<std::mutex> lg(m);
        std::cout << "Executing function from a " << param << '\n';
    } // lock_guard goes out of scope here and unlocks the mutex
}
```

```
int main()
{
    std::thread t1{ myfunction, "Thread 1" };
    std::thread t2{ myfunction, "Thread 2" };
    t1.join();
    t2.join();
}
```

Possible Output:

```
Executing function from a Thread 1
Executing function from a Thread 1
Executing function from a Thread 1
Executing function from a Thread 1
Executing function from a Thread 1
Executing function from a Thread 2
Executing function from a Thread 2
Executing function from a Thread 2
Executing function from a Thread 2
Executing function from a Thread 2
```

Deleted and Defaulted Functions

If we do not supply a default constructor, the compiler will generate one for us so that we can write

```
class MyClass
{
};

int main()
{
    MyClass o; // OK, there is an implicitly defined default constructor
}
```

However, in certain situations, the default constructor will not be implicitly generated. For example, when we define a copy constructor for our class, the default constructor is implicitly deleted. Example:

```cpp
#include <iostream>

class MyClass
{
public:
    MyClass(const MyClass& other)
    {
        std::cout << "Copy constructor invoked.";
    }
};

int main()
{
    MyClass o; // Error, there is no default constructor
}
```

To force the instantiation of a default, compiler-generated constructor, we provide the =*default* specifier in its declaration. Example:

```cpp
#include <iostream>

class MyClass
{
public:
    MyClass() = default; // defaulted member function

    MyClass(const MyClass& other)
    {
        std::cout << "Copy constructor invoked.";
    }
};

int main()
{
```

```
    MyClass o; // Now OK, the defaulted default constructor is there
    MyClass o2 = o; // Invoking the copy constructor
}
```

Output:

```
Copy constructor invoked.
```

The =*default* specifier, when used on a member function, means: whatever the language rules, I want this default member function to be there. I do not want it to be implicitly disabled.

Similarly, if we want to disable a member function from appearing, we use the =*delete* specifier. To disable the copy constructor and copy assignment, we would write

```
#include <iostream>

class MyClass
{
public:
    MyClass()
    {
        std::cout << "Default constructor invoked.";
    }

    MyClass(const MyClass& other) = delete; // delete the copy constructor

    MyClass& operator=(const MyClass& other) = delete; // delete the copy
// assignment operator
};

int main()
{
    MyClass o; // OK
    MyClass o2 = o; // Error, a call to deleted copy constructor
    MyClass o3;
    o3 = o; // Error, a call to the deleted copy assignment operator
}
```

These specifiers are mostly used in situations where we want to

    a.   Force the instantiation of implicitly defined member functions such as constructors and assignment operators when we use the *=default;* expression

    b.   Disable the instantiation of implicitly defined member functions using the *=delete;* expression

These expressions can also be used for other functions.

Type Aliases

A type alias is a user-provided name for the existing type. If we want to use a different name for the existing type, we write *using my_type_name = existing_type_name;*

    Example:

```
#include <iostream>
#include <string>
#include <vector>

using MyInt = int;
using MyString = std::string;
using MyVector = std::vector<int>;
int main()
{
    MyInt x = 123;
    MyString s = "Hello World";
    MyVector v = { 1, 2, 3, 4, 5 };
}
```

C++14

C++14 is an ISO C++ standard published in 2014. It brings some additions to the language and the standard library but mainly complements and fixes the C++11 standard. When we say we want to use the C++11 standard, what we actually want is the C++14 standard. The following are some of the new features for C++14.

To compile for C++14, add the *-std=c++14* flag to a command-line compilation string if using the g++ or clang compiler. In Visual Studio, choose *Project* ➤ *Options* ➤ *Configuration Properties* ➤ *C/C++* ➤ *Language* ➤ *C++ Language Standard* and choose *C++14*.

Binary Literals

Values are represented by literals. So far, we have mentioned three different kinds of binary literals – decimal, hexadecimal, and octal – as in the following example:

```
int main()
{
    int x = 10;
    int y = 0xA;
    int z = 012;
}
```

These three variables have the same value of 10, represented by different number literals. The C++14 standard introduces the fourth kind of integral literals called *binary literals*. Using binary literals, we can represent the value in its binary form. The literal has a 0b prefix, followed by a sequence of ones and zeros representing a value. To represent the number 10 as a binary literal, we write

```
int main()
{
    int x = 0b1010;
}
```

The famous number 42 in binary form would be

```
int main()
{
    int x = 0b101010;
}
```

Important to remember   Values are values; they are some sequence of bits and bytes in memory. What can be different is the value *representation*. There are decimal, hexadecimal, octal, and binary representations of the value. These different forms of the same thing can be relevant to us humans. To a machine, it is all bits and bytes, transistors, and electrical current.

Digit Separators

In C++14, we can separate digits with a single quote to make it more readable:

```cpp
int main()
{
    int x =100'000'000;
}
```

The compiler ignores the quotes. The separators are only here for our benefit, for example, to split a large number into more readable sections.

Auto for Functions

We can deduce the function type based on the return statement value:

```cpp
auto myintfn() // integer
{
    return 123;
}

auto mydoublefn() // double
{
    return 3.14;
}

int main()
{
    auto x = myintfn(); // int
    auto d = mydoublefn(); // double
}
```

Generic Lambdas

We can use auto parameters in lambda functions now. The type of the parameter will be deduced from the value supplied to a lambda function. This is also called a *generic lambda*:

```
#include <iostream>

int main()
{
    auto mylambda = [](auto p) {std::cout << "Lambda parameter: "
    << p << '\n'; };
    mylambda(123);
    mylambda(3.14);
}
```

Output:

```
Lambda parameter: 123
Lambda parameter: 3.14
```

std::make_unique

C++14 introduces a *std::make_unique* function for creating unique pointers. It is declared inside a <memory> header. Prefer this function to a raw new operator when creating unique pointers:

```
#include <iostream>
#include <memory>

class MyClass
{
private:
    int x;
    double d;
public:
    MyClass(int xx, double dd)
        : x{ xx }, d{ dd }    {}
```

```
    void printdata() { std::cout << "x: " << x << ", d: " << d; }
};

int main()
{
    auto p = std::make_unique<MyClass>(123, 456.789);
    p->printdata();
}
```

Output:

```
x: 123, d: 456.789
```

C++17

The C++17 standard introduces new language and library features and changes some of the language rules.

Nested Namespaces

Remember how we said we could have nested namespaces? We can put a namespace into another namespace. We used the following nested namespace syntax:

```
namespace MyNameSpace1
{
    namespace MyNameSpace2
    {
        namespace MyNameSpace3
        {
            // some code
        }
    }
}
```

The C++17 standard allows us to nest namespaces using the namespace resolution operator. The preceding example can now be rewritten as

```
namespace MyNameSpace1::MyNameSpace2::MyNameSpace3
{
    // some code
}
```

Constexpr Lambdas

Lambdas can now be a constant expression, meaning they can be evaluated during compile time:

```
int main()
{
    constexpr auto mylambda = [](int x, int y) { return x + y; };
    static_assert(mylambda(10, 20) == 30, "The lambda condition is not
    true.");
}
```

An equivalent example where we put the constexpr specifier in the lambda itself would be

```
int main()
{
    auto mylambda = [](int x, int y) constexpr { return x + y; };
    static_assert(mylambda(10, 20) == 30, "The lambda condition is not
    true.");
}
```

This was not the case in earlier C++ standards.

Structured Bindings

Structured binding binds the variable names to elements of compile-time known expressions, such as arrays or maps. If we want to have multiple variables taking values of expression elements, we use structured bindings. The syntax is

```
auto [myvar1, myvar2, myvar3] = some_expression;
```

A simple example where we bound three variables to be aliases for three array elements would be

```cpp
int main()
{
    int arr[] = { 1, 2, 3 };
    auto [myvar1, myvar2, myvar3] = arr;
}
```

Now we have defined three integer variables. These variables have array element values of 1, 2, and 3, respectively. These variables are copies of array elements. Making changes to variables does not affect the array elements themselves:

```cpp
#include <iostream>

int main()
{
    int arr[] = { 1, 2, 3 };
    auto [myvar1, myvar2, myvar3] = arr;
    myvar1 = 10;
    myvar2 = 20;
    myvar3 = 30;
    for (auto el : arr)
    {
        std::cout << el << ' ';
    }
}
```

Output:

---

1 2 3

We can make structured bindings of reference type by using the auto& syntax. This means the variables are now references to array elements and making changes to variables also changes the array elements:

```cpp
#include <iostream>

int main()
{
    int arr[] = { 1, 2, 3 };
    auto& [myvar1, myvar2, myvar3] = arr;
    myvar1 = 10;
    myvar2 = 20;
    myvar3 = 30;
    for (auto el : arr)
    {
        std::cout << el << ' ';
    }
}
```

Output:

```
10 20 30
```

It is an excellent way of introducing and binding multiple variables to some container-like expression elements.

std::filesystem

The std::filesystem library allows us to work with files, paths, and folders on our system. The library is declared through a <filesystem> header. Paths can represent paths to files and paths to folders. To check if a given folder exists, we use

```cpp
#include <iostream>
#include <filesystem>

int main()
{
    std::filesystem::path folderpath = "C:\\MyFolder\\";
    if (std::filesystem::exists(folderpath))
    {
        std::cout << "The path: " << folderpath << " exists.";
    }
```

```
    else
    {
        std::cout << "The path: " << folderpath << " does not exist.";
    }
}
```

Possible Output:

```
The path: "C:\\MyFolder\\" exists.
```

Similarly, we can use the std::filesystem::path object to check if a file exists:

```
#include <iostream>
#include <filesystem>

int main()
{
    std::filesystem::path folderpath = "C:\\MyFolder\\myfile.txt";
    if (std::filesystem::exists(folderpath))
    {
        std::cout << "The file: " << folderpath << " exists.";
    }
    else
    {
        std::cout << "The file: " << folderpath << " does not exist.";
    }
}
```

Possible Output:

```
The file: "C:\\MyFolder\\myfile.txt" does not exist.
```

To iterate over folder elements, we use the *std::filesystem::directory_iterator* iterator:

```
#include <iostream>
#include <filesystem>

int main()
{
```

```
    auto myfolder = "C:\\MyFolder\\";
    for (auto el : std::filesystem::directory_iterator(myfolder))
    {
        std::cout << el.path() << '\n';
    }
}
```

Possible Output:

```
"C:\\MyFolder\\My Subfolder 1"
"C:\\MyFolder\\My Subfolder 1 - Copy"
"C:\\MyFolder\\My Subfolder 1 - Copy (2)"
"C:\\MyFolder\\My Subfolder 1 - Copy (3)"
```

Here, we iterate over the directory entries and print every element's full path using the *.path()* member function.

For Linux, we need to adjust the path and use the following instead:

```
#include <iostream>
#include <filesystem>

int main()
{
    auto myfolder = "MyFolder/";
    for (auto el : std::filesystem::directory_iterator(myfolder))
    {
        std::cout << el.path() << '\n';
    }
}
```

Possible Output:

```
"MyFolder/My Subfolder 1 - Copy (2)"
"MyFolder/My Subfolder 1 - Copy"
"MyFolder/My Subfolder 1 - Copy (3)"
"MyFolder/My Subfolder 1"
```

To iterate over folder elements recursively, we use the *std::filesystem::recursive_directory_iterator*. This allows us to iterate recursively over all subfolders in a folder. On Windows, we would use

```
#include <iostream>
#include <filesystem>

int main()
{
    auto myfolder = "C:\\MyFolder\\";
    for (auto el : std::filesystem::recursive_directory_iterator(myfolder))
    {
        std::cout << el.path() << '\n';
    }
}
```

Possible Output:

```
"C:\\MyFolder\\My Subfolder 1"
"C:\\MyFolder\\My Subfolder 1 - Copy"
"C:\\MyFolder\\My Subfolder 1 - Copy (2)"
"C:\\MyFolder\\My Subfolder 1 - Copy (3)"
"C:\\MyFolder\\My Subfolder 1 - Copy (3)\\My File.txt"
"C:\\MyFolder\\My Subfolder 1 - Copy (3)\\My Other File.txt"
```

On Linux and similar OSes, we would use the following path:

```
#include <iostream>
#include <filesystem>

int main()
{
    auto myfolder = "MyFolder/";
    for (auto el : std::filesystem::recursive_directory_iterator (myfolder))
    {
        std::cout << el.path() << '\n';
    }
}
```

Possible Output:

```
"MyFolder/My Subfolder 1 - Copy (2)"
"MyFolder/My Subfolder 1 - Copy"
"MyFolder/My Subfolder 1 - Copy (3)"
"MyFolder/My Subfolder 1 - Copy (3)/My Other File.txt"
"MyFolder/My Subfolder 1 - Copy (3)/My File.txt"
"MyFolder/My Subfolder 1"
```

The following are some useful utility functions inside the std::filesystem namespace:

- `std::filesystem::create_directory` for creating a directory

- `std::filesystem::copy` for copying files and directories

- `std::filesystem::remove` for removing a file or an empty folder

- `std::filesystem::remove_all` for removing folders and subfolders

std::string_view

Copying data can be an expensive operation in terms of CPU usage. Passing substrings as function parameters would require making a copy of substrings. This is a costly operation. The string_view class template is an attempt to rectify that.

The string_view is a non-owning view of a string or a substring. It is a reference to something that is already there in the memory. It is implemented as a pointer to some character sequence plus the size of that sequence. With this kind of structure, we can parse strings efficiently.

The std::string_view is declared inside the `<string_view>` header file. To create a string_view from an existing string, we write

```cpp
#include <iostream>
#include <string>
#include <string_view>

int main()
{
```

```
    std::string s = "Hello World from a string view.";
    std::string_view sw(s);
    std::cout << sw;
}
```

Output:

```
Hello World from a string view.
```

To create a string_view for a substring of the first five characters, we use the different constructor overload. This string_view constructor takes a pointer to the first string element and the length of the substring:

```
#include <iostream>
#include <string>
#include <string_view>

int main()
{
    std::string s = "Hello World from a string view.";
    std::string_view sw(s.c_str() , 5);
    std::cout << sw;
}
```

Output:

```
Hello
```

Once we create a string_view, we can use its member functions. To create a substring out of a string_view, we use the .substr() member function. To create a substring, we supply the starting position index and length. To create a substring of the first five characters, we use

```
#include <iostream>
#include <string>
#include <string_view>

int main()
{
```

```
    std::string s = "Hello World";
    std::string_view sw(s);
    std::cout << sw.substr(0, 5);
}
```

Output:

```
Hello
```

A string_view allows us to parse (not change) the data that is already in the memory without having to make copies of the data. This data is owned by another string or character array object.

std::any

The *std::any* container can hold a single value of any type. This container is declared inside the header file. Example:

```
#include <any>

int main()
{
    std::any a = 345.678;
    std::any b = true;
    std::any c = 123;
}
```

To access the value of a *std::any* object in a safe manner, we cast it to a type of our choice using the *std::any_cast* function:

```
#include <iostream>
#include <any>

int main()
{
    std::any a = 123;
    std::cout << "Any accessed as an integer: " << std::any_cast<int>(a)
    << '\n';
    a = 456.789;
```

317

```
std::cout << "Any accessed as a double: " << std::any_cast<double>(a)
<< '\n';
a = true;
std::cout << "Any accessed as a boolean: " << std::any_cast<bool>(a)
<< '\n';
}
```

Output:

```
Any accessed as an integer: 123
Any accessed as a double: 456.789
Any accessed as a boolean: 1
```

Important, the *std::any_cast* will throw an exception if we try to convert, for example, 123 to type double. This function performs only type-safe conversions. Another *std::any* member function is *.has_value()* which checks if the *std::any* object holds a value:

```
#include <iostream>
#include <any>

int main()
{
    std::any a = 123;
    if (a.has_value())
    {
        std::cout << "Object a contains a value." << '\n';
    }
    std::any b{};
    if (b.has_value())
    {
        std::cout << "Object b contains a value." << '\n';
    }
    else
    {
        std::cout << "Object b does not contain a value." << '\n';
    }
}
```

Output:

```
Object a contains a value.
Object b does not contain a value.
```

---

std::variant

There is another type of data in C++ called *union*. A union is a type whose data members of different types occupy the same memory. Only one data member can be accessed at a time. The size of a union in memory is the size of its largest data member. The data members overlap in a sense. To define a union type in C++, we write

```
union MyUnion
{
    char c;         // one byte
    int x;          // four bytes
    double d;       // eight bytes
};
```

Here, we declared a union type that can hold characters or integers or doubles. The size of this union is the size of its largest data member double, which is probably eight bytes, depending on the implementation. Although the union declares multiple data members, it can only hold a value of one member at any given time. This is because all the data members share the same memory location. And we can only access the member that was the last written to. Example:

```
#include <iostream>

union MyUnion
{
    char c;         // one byte
    int x;          // four bytes
    double d;       // eight bytes
};
```

```
int main()
{
    MyUnion o;
    o.c = 'A';
    std::cout << o.c << '\n';
    // accessing o.x or o.d is undefined behavior at this point
    o.x = 123;
    std::cout << o.c;
    // accessing o.c or o.d is undefined behavior at this point
    o.d = 456.789;
    std::cout << o.c;
    // accessing o.c or o.x is undefined behavior at this point
}
```

Possible Output:

A
{⊣

C++17 introduces a new way of working with unions using the *std::variant* class template from a *<variant>* header. This class template offers a type-safe way of storing and accessing a union. To declare a variant using a *std::variant*, we would write

```
#include <variant>

int main()
{
    std::variant<char, int, double> myvariant;
}
```

This example defines a variant that can hold three types. When we initialize or assign a value to a variant, an appropriate type is chosen. For example, if we initialize a variant with a character value, the variant will currently hold a char data member. Accessing other members at this point will throw an exception. Example:

```cpp
#include <iostream>
#include <variant>

int main()
{
    std::variant<char, int, double> myvariant{ 'a' }; // variant now holds
    // a char
    std::cout << std::get<0>(myvariant) << '\n'; // obtain a data member by
    // index
    std::cout << std::get<char>(myvariant) << '\n'; // obtain a data member
    // by type
    myvariant = 1024; // variant now holds an int
    std::cout << std::get<1>(myvariant) << '\n'; // by index
    std::cout << std::get<int>(myvariant) << '\n'; // by type
    myvariant = 123.456; // variant now holds a double
}
```

Output:

```
a
a
1024
1024
```

We can access a variant value by index using the *std::get<index_number>(variant_name)* function. Or we can access the variant value by a type name using *std::get<type_name>(variant_name)*. If we tried to access a wrong type or wrong index member, an exception of type *const std::bad_variant_access&* would be raised. Example:

```cpp
#include <iostream>
#include <variant>

int main()
{
    std::variant<int, double> myvariant{ 123 }; // variant now holds an int
    std::cout << "Current variant: " << std::get<int>(myvariant) << '\n';
    try
```

```
    {
        std::cout << std::get<double>(myvariant) << '\n'; // exception is
        // raised
    }
    catch (const std::bad_variant_access& ex)
    {
        std::cout << "Exception raised. Description: " << ex.what();
    }
}
```

Output:

```
Current variant: 123
Exception raised. Description: bad variant access
```

We define a variant that can hold either int or double. We initialize the variant with a 123 literal of type int. So now our variant holds an int data member. We can access that member using the index of 0 or a type name that we supply to the std::get function. Then we try to access the wrong data member of type double. An exception is raised. And the particular type of that exception *is std::bad_variant_access*. In the catch block, we handle the exception by parsing the parameter we named *ex*. A parameter is of type *std::bad_variant_access,* which has a *.what()* member function that provides a short description of the exception.

C++20

The C++20 standard promises to bring some big additions to the language. Its impact on the existing standards is said to be as big as the C++11 was on a C++98/C++03 standard. Some of the following things may, at first glance, seem intimidating, especially when beginning C++. However, do not worry. At the time of writing, none of the compilers fully support the C++20 standard, but that is about to change. Once the compilers fully support the C++20 standard, trying out the examples will be much easier. With that in mind, let us go through some of the most exciting C++20 features.

Modules

Modules are the new C++20 feature, which aims to eliminate the need for the separation of code into header and source files. So far, in traditional C++, we have organized our source code using header and source files. We keep our declarations/interfaces in header files. We put our definitions/implementations in source files. For example, we have a header file with a function declaration:

mylibrary.h

```
#ifndef MYLIBRARY_H
#define MYLIBRARY_H
int myfunction();
#endif // !MYLIBRARY_H
```

Here, we declare a function called `myfunction()`. We surround the code with header guards, which ensure the header file is not included multiple times during the compilation. And we have a source file with the function definition. This source file includes our header file:

mylibrary.cpp:

```
#include "mylibrary.h"

int myfunction()
{
    return 123;
}
```

In our *main.cpp* file, we also include the preceding header file and call the function:

```
#include "mylibrary.h"

int main()
{
    int x = myfunction();
}
```

We include the same header multiple times. This increases compilation time. Modules are included only once, and we do not have to separate the code into interface and implementation. One way is to have a single module file, for example, *mymodule. cpp,* where we provide the entire implementation and export of this function.

To create a simple module file that implements and exports the preceding function, we write

mymodule.cpp:

```
export module mymodule;
export int myfunction() { return 123; }
```

Explanation: The `export module mymodule;` statement says there is a module called *mymodule* in this file. In the second line, the *export* specifier on the function means the function will be visible once the module is imported into the main program.

We include the module in our main program by writing the `import mymodule;` statement.

main.cpp:

```
import mymodule;

int main()
{
    int x = myfunction();
}
```

In our main program, we import the module and call the exported `myfunction()` function.

A module can also provide an implementation but does need to export it. If we do not want our function to be visible to the main program, we will omit the export specifier in the module. This makes the implementation private to the module:

```
export module mymodule;
export int myfunction() { return 123; }
int myprivatefunction() { return 456; }
```

If we have a module with a namespace in it, and a declaration inside that namespace is exported, the entire namespace is exported. Within that namespace, only the exported functions are visible. Example:

mymodule2.cpp:

```
export module mymodule2;

namespace MyModule
{
    export int myfunction() { return 123; }
}
```

main2.cpp:

```
import mymodule2;

int main()
{
    int x = MyModule::myfunction();
}
```

Concepts

Remember the class templates and function templates providing generic types T? If we want our template argument T to satisfy certain requirements, then we use concepts. In other words, we want our T to satisfy certain compile-time criteria. The signature for a concept is

```
template <typename T>
concept concept_name = requires (T var_name) { requirement_expression; };
```

The second line defines a concept name followed by a reserved word `requires`, followed by an optional template argument T and a local var_name, followed by a `requirement_expression` which is a constexpr of type bool.

In a nutshell, the concept predicate specifies the requirements a template argument must satisfy in order to be used in a template. Some of the requirements we can write ourselves, and some are already premade.

We can say that concepts constrain types to certain requirements. They can also be seen as a sort of compile-time assertions for our template types.

For example, if we want a template argument to be incrementable by one, we will specify the concept for it:

```
template <typename T>
concept MustBeIncrementable = requires (T x) { x += 1; };
```

To use this concept in a template, we write

```
template<MustBeIncrementable T>
void myfunction(T x)
{
    // code goes in here
}
```

Another way to include the concept in our template is

```
template<typename T> requires MustBeIncrementable <T>
void myfunction(T x)
{
    // code goes in here
}
```

A full working example would be

```
#include <iostream>
#include <concepts>

template <typename T>
concept MustBeIncrementable = requires (T x) { x ++; };

template<MustBeIncrementable T>
void myfunction(T x)
{
    x += 1;
    std::cout << x << '\n';
}
```

```
int main()
{
    myfunction<char>(96); // OK
    myfunction<int>(123); // OK
    myfunction<double>(345.678); // OK
}
```

Output:

---

a

124

346.678

This concept ensures our argument x of type T must be able to accept operator ++, and the argument must be able to be incremented by one. This check is performed during the compile time. The requirement is indeed true for types char, int, and double. If we used a type for which the requirement is not fulfilled, the compiler would issue a compile-time error.

We can combine multiple concepts. Let us, for example, have a concept that requires the T argument to be an even or an odd number:

```
template <typename T>
concept SupportsModulo = requires (T x) { x % 2; };
```

Now our template can include both the MustBeIncrementable and SupportsModulo concepts:

```
template<typename T> requires MustBeIncrementable<T> &&
MustBeEvenNumber<T>;
void myfunction(T x)
{
    // code goes in here
}
```

The keyword requires is used both for the expression in the concept and when including the concept into our template class/function.

The complete program, which includes both concept requirements, would be

```
#include <iostream>
#include <concepts>

template <typename T>
concept MustBeIncrementable = requires (T x) { x++; };
template <typename T>
concept SupportsModulo = requires (T x) { x % 2; };

template<typename T> requires MustBeIncrementable<T> && SupportsModulo<T>
void myfunction(T x)
{
    std::cout << "The value conforms to both conditions: " << x << '\n';
}

int main()
{
    myfunction<char>(123); // OK
    myfunction<int>(124); // OK
    myfunction<double>(345); // Error, a floating point number is not even
    // nor odd
}
```

In this example, the template will be instantiated if both concept requirements
are evaluated to be true during compile time. Only the myfunction<char>(123); and
myfunction<int>(124); functions can be instantiated and pass the compilation. The
arguments of types char and int are indeed incrementable and can be either even or odd.
However, the statement myfunction<double>(345); does not pass a compilation. The
reason is that the second requirement SupportsModulo is not fulfilled, as floating-point
numbers are neither odd nor even.

Important! Both concepts say for every x of type T, the statement inside the code
block { } compiles and nothing more. It just compiles. If it compiles, the requirement for
that type is fulfilled.

If we want our type T to have a member function, for example, .empty(), and we want
the result of that function to be convertible to type bool, we write

```
template <typename T>
concept HasMemberFunction requires (T x)
{
    { x.empty() } -> std::convertible_to(bool);
};
```

There are multiple predefined concepts in the C++20 standard. They check if the type fulfills certain requirements. These predefined concepts are located inside the <concepts> header. Some of them are

    a.   `std::integral` – Specifies that the type should be an integral type

    b.   `std::boolean` – Specifies the type that can be used as a boolean type

    c.   `std::move_constructible` – Specifies that the object of a particular type can be constructed using the move semantics

    d.   `std::movable` – Specifies that the object of a certain type T can be moved

    e.   `std::signed_integral` – Says the type is both integral and a signed integral

Lambda Templates

We can now use template syntax in our lambda functions. Example:

```
auto mylambda = []<typename T>(T param)
{
    // code
};
```

For example, to print out the generic type names using a templated lambda expression, we would write

```
#include <iostream>
#include <vector>
#include <typeinfo>
```

```
int main()
{
    auto mylambda = []<typename T>(T param)
    {
        std::cout << typeid(T).name() << '\n';
    };
    std::vector<int> v = { 1, 2, 3, 4, 5 };
    mylambda(v); // integer
    std::vector<double> v2 = { 3.14, 123.456, 7.13 };
    mylambda(v2); // double
}
```

   Output:

```
class std::vector<int,class std::allocator<int> >
class std::vector<double,class std::allocator<double> >
```

[likely] and [unlikely] Attributes

If we know that some paths of execution are more likely to be executed than others, we can help the compiler optimize the code by placing *attributes*. We use the *[[likely]]* attribute before the statement that is more likely to be executed. We can also put the *[[unlikely]]* attribute before the statement that is unlikely to be executed. For example, the attributes can be used on *case* branches inside the *switch* statement:

```
#include <iostream>

void mychoice(int i)
{
    switch (i)
    {
    [[likely]] case 1:
        std::cout << "Likely to be executed.";
        break;
    [[unlikely]] case 2:
        std::cout << "Unlikely to be executed.";
        break;
```

```
        default:
            break;
    }
}

int main()
{
    mychoice(1);
}
```

Output:

```
Likely to be executed.
```

If we want to use these attributes on the if-else branches, we write

```
#include <iostream>

int main()
{
    bool choice = true;
    if (choice) [[likely]]
    {
        std::cout << "This statement is likely to be executed.";
    }
    else [[unlikely]]
    {
        std::cout << "This statement is unlikely to be executed.";
    }
}
```

Output:

```
This statement is likely to be executed.
```

Ranges

A range, in general, is an object that refers to a range of elements. The new C++20 ranges feature is declared inside a <ranges> header. The ranges themselves are accessed via the *std::ranges* name. With classic containers such as a std::vector, if we want to sort the data, we would use

```cpp
#include <iostream>
#include <vector>
#include <algorithm>

int main()
{
    std::vector<int> v = { 1, 2, 3, 4, 5 };
    std::sort(v.begin(), v.end());
    for (auto el : v)
    {
        std::cout << el << '\n';
    }
}
```

Output:

```
1
2
3
4
5
```

The std::sort function accepts the vector's *.begin()* and *end()* iterators. With ranges, it is much simpler. We just provide the name of the range without iterators:

```cpp
#include <iostream>
#include <ranges>
#include <vector>
#include <algorithm>
```

```
int main()
{
    std::vector<int> v = { 3, 5, 2, 1, 4 };
    std::ranges::sort(v);
    for (auto el : v)
    {
        std::cout << el << '\n';
    }
}
```

Output:

1

2

3

4

5

Ranges have a feature called adaptors. One of the range adaptors is *views*. The views adaptors are accessed via std::ranges::views. Views are *non-owning*. They cannot change the values of the underlying elements. It is also said they are *lazily executed*. This means the code from the views adaptors will not be executed until we iterate over the result of such views.

Let us create an example that uses range views to filter out even numbers and print only the odd numbers from a vector by creating a range view:

```
#include <iostream>
#include <ranges>
#include <vector>
#include <algorithm>

int main()
{
    std::vector<int> v = { 1, 2, 3, 4, 5 };
    auto oddnumbersview = v | std::views::filter([](int x) { return x % 2
    == 1; });
    for (auto el : oddnumbersview)
```

```
    {
        std::cout << el << '\n';
    }
}
```

Output:

```
1
3
5
```

Explanation: We have a simple vector with some elements. Then we create a view range adaptor on that vector, which filters the numbers in the range. For this, we use the pipe operator |. Only the numbers for which the predicate is true are included. In our case, this means the even numbers are excluded. Then we iterate over the filtered view and print out the elements.

It's important to note that the underlying vector's elements are unaffected as we are operating on a view, not on a vector.

Let us create an example that creates a view that returns only numbers greater than two:

```
#include <iostream>
#include <ranges>
#include <vector>
#include <algorithm>

int main()
{
    std::vector<int> v = { 1, 2, 3, 4, 5 };
    auto greaterthan2view = v | std::views::filter([](int x) { return x
    > 2; });
    for (auto el : greaterthan2view)
    {
        std::cout << el << '\n';
    }
}
```

Output:

3

4

5

Now, let us combine the two views into one big view by separating them with multiple pipe | operators:

```cpp
#include <iostream>
#include <ranges>
#include <vector>
#include <algorithm>

int main()
{
    std::vector<int> v = { 1, 2, 3, 4, 5 };
    auto oddandgreaterthan2 = v | std::views::filter([](int x) { return x %
    2 == 1; })
                                | std::views::filter([](int x) { return x
                                > 2; });
    for (auto el : oddandgreaterthan2)
    {
        std::cout << el << '\n';
    }
}
```

Output:

3

5

This example creates a view range adaptor containing odd numbers greater than two. We create this view by combining two different range views into one.

Other range adaptors are *algorithms*. The idea is to have the algorithms overload for ranges. To call an algorithm adaptor, we use std::ranges::algorithm_ name(parameters).

335

Example using the std::ranges::reverse() algorithm:

```cpp
#include <iostream>
#include <ranges>
#include <vector>
#include <algorithm>

int main()
{
    std::vector<int> v = { 1, 2, 3, 4, 5 };
    std::ranges::reverse(v);
    for (auto el : v)
    {
        std::cout << el << '\n';
    }
}
```

Output:

```
5
4
3
2
1
```

Unlike views, the ranges algorithms modify the actual vector content.

Coroutines

A coroutine is a function that can be suspended and resumed. The ordinary function is a coroutine if it uses any of the following operators in its function body:

f. co_await – Suspends the execution of the coroutine until some other computation is performed, that is, until the coroutine itself resumes

g. co_yield – Suspends a coroutine and returns a value to the caller

h. co_return – Returns from a coroutine and stops its execution

std::span

Some containers and types store their elements in a sequence, one next to the other. This is the case for arrays and vectors. We can represent such containers with a pointer to their first element plus the length of the container. A *std::span* class template from a ** header is just that – a reference to a span of contiguous container elements. One reason to use the *std::span* is that it is cheap to construct and copy. A span does not own a vector or an array it references. However, it can change the value of the elements. To create a span from a vector, we use

```
#include <iostream>
#include <vector>
#include <span>

int main()
{
    std::vector<int> v = { 1, 2, 3 };
    std::span<int> myintspan = v;
    myintspan[2] = 256;
    for (auto el : v)
    {
        std::cout << el << '\n';
    }
}
```

Output:

```
1
2
256
```

Here, we created a span that references vector elements. Then we used the span to change the vector's third element. With span, we do not have to worry about passing a pointer and a length around, and we just use the neat syntax of a span wrapper. Since the size of the vector can change, we say our span has a *dynamic extent*. We can create a fixed-size span from a fixed-size array. We say our span now has a *static extent*. Example:

```
#include <iostream>
#include <span>

int main()
{
    int arr[] = { 1, 2, 3, 4, 5 };
    std::span<int, 5> myintspan = arr;
    myintspan[4] = 10;
    for (auto el : arr)
    {
        std::cout << el << '\n';
    }
}
```

Output:

```
1
2
3
4
10
```

Mathematical Constants

The C++20 standard introduces a way to represent some of the mathematical constants. To use them, we need to include the *<numbers>* header. The constants themselves are inside the *std::numbers* namespace. The following example shows how to use numbers *pi* and *e*, the results of logarithmic functions, and the square roots of numbers 2 and 3:

```
#include <iostream>
#include <numbers>

int main()
{
    std::cout << "Pi: " << std::numbers::pi << '\n';
    std::cout << "e: " << std::numbers::e << '\n';
    std::cout << "log2(e): " << std::numbers::log2e << '\n';
```

```cpp
    std::cout << "log10(e): " << std::numbers::log10e << '\n';
    std::cout << "ln(2): " << std::numbers::ln2 << '\n';
    std::cout << "ln(10): " << std::numbers::ln10 << '\n';
    std::cout << "sqrt(2): " << std::numbers::sqrt2 << '\n';
    std::cout << "sqrt(3): " << std::numbers::sqrt3 << '\n';
}
```

Output:

```
Pi: 3.14159
e: 2.71828
log2(e): 1.4427
log10(e): 0.434294
ln(2): 0.693147
ln(10): 2.30259
sqrt(2): 1.41421
sqrt(3): 1.73205
```

C++23

The C++23 is a C++ standard following the C++20 standard. Compared to C++20, the C++23 standard introduces fewer new features. The standard is yet to be officially published at the time of writing.

To compile for the C++23 standard using GCC, currently, we supply the -std=c++2b flag to our g++ compilation string:

```
g++ -std=c++2b source.cpp
```

In Visual Studio, we choose Project ➤ Project Properties ➤ C/C++ ➤ Language, and in the C++ Language Standard, we choose the Preview ➤ Features from the Latest C++ Working Draft option, which will eventually be renamed to ISO C++23 Standard.

Let us look at some of the C++23 language and standard library features.

Multidimensional Subscript Operator

Up to C++23, if we wanted to access a multidimensional array element, let us say in a two-dimensional array, we had to use the following syntax:

```
myarr[x_index][y_index];
```

Before C++23, if we wanted to access an array element in a three-dimensional array, we would write

```
myarr[x_index][y_index][z_index];
```

Starting with the C++23, we can use the multidimensional subscript operator [ ], inside which we provide comma-separated indexes:

```
myarr[x_index, y_index];
```

For a three-dimensional array, the C++23 syntax would be

```
myarr[x_index, y_index, z_index];
```

The syntax for overloading a multidimensional subscript operator for a class is simple:

```
MyClass& operator[](size_t dimension_1, size_t dimension_2, etc... )
noexcept {
    // code
}
```

Literal Suffixes for size_t

Before C++23, we had several integer literal suffixes such as u, l, ul, ll, etc. These literal suffixes made the literals of a certain type. Example:

```
auto x1 = 123u; // unsigned
auto x2 = 123l; // long
auto x3 = 123ul; // unsigned long
auto x4 = 123ll; // long long
```

Starting with C++23, we have the uz literal suffix, which makes a literal of type std::size_t. Example:

```
auto x5 = 123uz; // std::size_t
```

And we also have the z literal, which makes the literal of the signed integer type corresponding to the std::size_t type. Example:

```
auto x6 = 123z; // the signed integer type corresponding to
std::size_t type
```

The #warning Preprocessor Directive

We can now issue a custom, user-defined warning or diagnostic message without interrupting the translation process using the #warning preprocessor directive.

The #warning directive has the following syntax: #warning "Custom warning message".

Example:

```
#include <iostream>

#warning "User-defined warning message."
#warning "Some diagnostics message."

int main()
{
    std::cout << "Custom warning messages issued without interrupting the
    compilation.";
}
```

This example compiles and runs, but the custom warning is issued during the translation/compilation process.

The std::string::contains() Member Function

Starting with the C++23 standard, the std::string type now has the .contains("given substring") member function.

This function checks if the string contains a given substring and returns the value of true if the string contains the given substring and false otherwise.

Prior to C++23, if we wanted to check if a string contained a given substring, we had to use the .find() member function and inspect its return value against the special value of std::string::npos.

The pre-C++23 example:

```cpp
#include <iostream>
#include <string>

int main()
{
    std::string s = "Hello World!";
    if (s.find("World") != std::string::npos)
    {
        std::cout << "The string contains the given substring." << '\n';
    }
    else
    {
        std::cout << "The string does not contain the given substring."
        << '\n';
    }
}
```

Output:

```
The string contains the given substring.
```

The easier, more readable C++23 example is

```cpp
#include <iostream>
#include <string>

int main()
{
    std::string s = "Hello World!";
    if (s.contains("World"))
    {
        std::cout << "The string contains the given substring." << '\n';
    }
```

```
    else
    {
        std::cout << "The string does not contain the given substring."
        << '\n';
    }
}
```

Output:

```
The string contains the given substring.
```

---

std::print

The `std::print` function prints the format string to a standard output or a file. The function is defined inside the `<print>` header file and has the following syntax:

```
std::print(<destination>, formatting_string, arguments);
```

The destination can be a standard output or a file. The formatting string is a sequence of symbols that will become a formatted output for a string and the arguments' values (for more info on the actual formatting rules, look to `std::format` and `std::formatter`).

The formatting string has a placeholder for the argument, marked by { }. The placeholder will be the position of the argument's formatted value. To print out a simple "Hello World." message, we write:

```
#include <print>

int main()
{
    std::print("Hello World.");
}
```

Output:

```
Hello World.
```

To print out the value of a single integer variable, we write:

```cpp
#include <print>

int main()
{
    int x = 123;
    std::print("The value of x is {}.", x);
}
```

Output:

```
The value of x is 123.
```

To print out the values of, for example, two variables, we write:

```cpp
#include <print>

int main()
{
    int x = 123;
    int y = 456;
    std::print("The x is {}, and the y is {}.", x, y);
}
```

Output:

```
The x is 123, and the y is 456.
```

The `std::print` is also capable of formatted print of built-in containers such as vectors, sets, maps, etc. There is also a `std::println` variant that adds a new line character at the end of a formatting string.

Other C++23 Features

There are also other C++23 features whose detailed description is beyond the scope of an introductory C++ course, so we will briefly mention their names: deducing `this`, `auto(x)`, assumptions, `std::flatmap`, `std::flatset`, and `std::stacktrace::current`.

When starting to learn C++, the choice of the C++ standard used is largely irrelevant (as long as we have at least C++11 in mind).

Congratulations on completing this chapter. Now we can move on to creating a couple of projects and put the knowledge gained so far into good use. Let us start.

CHAPTER 41

Projects

In this chapter, we will create a couple of C++ source code projects. We will start with a blank sheet and build our projects from the ground up, one code snippet at a time. The projects will increase in complexity as we progress through the code. Let us get started.

Project I: Book Inventory

Write a program that manages a book inventory. Requirements:

- Create a Book class with basic functionality (two data members, two constructors, a couple of getters and setters, and an arbitrary utility member function).

- In function main, create a single instance of a Book class using a default constructor.

- In function main, create a single instance of a Book class using a user-provided constructor and invoke the member functions.

- In function main, create a container of multiple Book objects using std::vector.

- Iterate through a container and invoke at least one member function.

First, we will create an empty project skeleton and include the appropriate header files, such as <iostream> for outputting the data, <vector> for storing the data in the function main, and <string> for working with std::string data members. The *source. cpp* file now looks like this:

```
#include <iostream>
#include <vector>
#include <string>
```

© Slobodan Dmitrović 2023
S. Dmitrović, *Modern C++ for Absolute Beginners*, https://doi.org/10.1007/978-1-4842-9274-7_41

```
class Book
{

};

int main()
{

}
```

Now, let us add a few data member fields that will describe the book better. For example, we can create a member field called `title` of type `std::string` and `pages` of type `int`. Both member fields will be placed inside the `private:` class section. Our listing now looks like the following:

```
#include <iostream>
#include <vector>
#include <string>

class Book
{
private:
    std::string title;
    int pages;
};

int main()
{

}
```

Let us now add a declaration for a single default constructor. The constructor will go into the `public` section. Listing:

```
#include <iostream>
#include <vector>
#include <string>

class Book
{
```

```
private:
    std::string title;
    int pages;
public:
    Book();
};

int main()
{

}
```

Let us define this default constructor outside the class. This constructor will initialize title and pages data members to hard-coded default values:

```
#include <iostream>
#include <vector>
#include <string>

class Book
{
private:
    std::string title;
    int pages;
public:
    Book();
};

Book::Book() : title{ "Default Book Title" }, pages{ 0 }
{
}

int main()
{

}
```

This constructor would be invoked when we want to create an object with no parameters. In the function main, let us create an object of type Book whose data members will have default values. The title would default to *"Default Book Title,"* and the number of pages will be set to zero. Listing:

```
#include <iostream>
#include <vector>
#include <string>

class Book
{
private:
    std::string title;
    int pages;
public:
    Book();
};

Book::Book() : title{ "Default Book Title" }, pages{ 0 }
{
}

int main()
{
    Book defaultbook;
    std::cout << "Default constructor invoked." << '\n';
}
```

Output:

```
Default constructor invoked.
```

Let us now add a second, user-provided constructor declaration that accepts two arguments. Listing:

```
#include <iostream>
#include <vector>
#include <string>
```

```
class Book
{
private:
    std::string title;
    int pages;
public:
    Book();
    Book(const std::string& atitle, int apages);
};

Book::Book() : title{ "Default Book Title" }, pages{ 0 }
{
}

int main()
{
    Book defaultbook;
    std::cout << "Default constructor invoked." << '\n';
}
```

Now, let us add the second constructor's definition outside the body of a class and use the constructor's initializer list to initialize data members with arguments:

```
#include <iostream>
#include <vector>
#include <string>

class Book
{
private:
    std::string title;
    int pages;
public:
    Book();
    Book(const std::string& atitle, int apages);
};

Book::Book() : title{ "Default Book Title" }, pages{ 0 }
```

```
{
}
```

**Book::Book(const std::string& atitle, int apages) : title{ atitle }, pages{
apages }**

```
{
}

int main()
{
    Book defaultbook;
    std::cout << "Default constructor invoked." << '\n';
}
```

In function main, we can invoke this second constructor and provide a custom book title and a custom number of pages. Listing:

```
#include <iostream>
#include <vector>
#include <string>

class Book
{
private:
    std::string title;
    int pages;
public:
    Book();
    Book(const std::string& atitle, int apages);
};

Book::Book() : title{ "Default Book Title" }, pages{ 0 }
{
}

Book::Book(const std::string& atitle, int apages) : title{ atitle }, pages{
apages }
{
}
```

```
int main()
{
    Book defaultbook;
    std::cout << "Default constructor invoked." << '\n';
    Book mybook{ "My Book Title", 123 };
    std::cout << "User-provided constructor invoked." << '\n';
}
```

Output:

```
Default constructor invoked.
User-provided constructor invoked.
```

Next, we will add a member function called void printdata(). This function will print out the values of both data members, title and pages. Let us pick up the pace and implement the function declaration inside the class, function definition outside the class, and function calls in the main program. Listing:

```
#include <iostream>
#include <vector>
#include <string>

class Book
{
private:
    std::string title;
    int pages;
public:
    Book();
    Book(const std::string& atitle, int apages);
    void printdata();
};

Book::Book() : title{ "Default Book Title" }, pages{ 0 }
{
}
```

```
Book::Book(const std::string& atitle, int apages) : title{ atitle }, pages{
apages }
{
}
```

```cpp
void Book::printdata()
{
    std::cout << "The book title is: " << title << ", and the number of
    pages is: " << pages << '\n';
}
```

```cpp
int main()
{
    Book defaultbook;
    std::cout << "Default constructor invoked." << '\n';

    Book mybook{ "My Book Title", 123 };
    std::cout << "User-provided constructor invoked." << '\n';
    mybook.printdata();
}
```

Output:

```
Default constructor invoked.
User-provided constructor invoked.
The book title is: My Book Title, and the number of pages is: 123
```

Let us add two getter functions (member functions that get/return the values of appropriate data members). One function is for returning the title, which we will call gettitle(), and one function is for returning the number of pages, called getpages(). Both getter functions will be marked as const, thus promising not to change any data members' values. The types of these functions will match the types of appropriate data members. In the next listing, we will implement the declarations, definitions, and function calls in the main. Listing:

```cpp
#include <iostream>
#include <vector>
#include <string>
```

```cpp
class Book
{
private:
    std::string title;
    int pages;
public:
    Book();
    Book(const std::string& atitle, int apages);
    void printdata();
    std::string gettitle() const;
    int getpages() const;
};

Book::Book() : title{ "Default Book Title" }, pages{ 0 }
{
}

Book::Book(const std::string& atitle, int apages) : title{ atitle },
pages{ apages }
{
}

void Book::printdata()
{
    std::cout << "The book title is: " << title << ", and the number of
    pages is: " << pages << '\n';
}

std::string Book::gettitle() const
{
    return title;
}

int Book::getpages() const
{
    return pages;
}
```

```
int main()
{
    Book defaultbook;
    std::cout << "Default constructor invoked." << '\n';

    Book mybook{ "My Book Title", 123 };
    std::cout << "User-provided constructor invoked." << '\n';
    mybook.printdata();

    std::cout << "The book title is: " << mybook.gettitle() << '\n';
    std::cout << "The number of pages is: " << mybook.getpages() << '\n';
}
```

Output:

```
Default constructor invoked.
User-provided constructor invoked.
The book title is: My Book Title, and the number of pages is: 123
The book title is: My Book Title
The number of pages is: 123
```

Since we have two getter functions, we can now implement two setter functions. Setter functions are member functions that simply set the value of appropriate data members using the argument provided. We will call them void settitle(const std::string& atitle) and void setpages(int apages). Both setter functions accept a single parameter. The first function accepts an argument by const reference because its std::string is a complex type, and we want to avoid creating unnecessary copies. The second function can accept a parameter by value because it is a simple, built-in type int. We will use these parameters to set/overwrite the values of appropriate data members. The function declarations, definitions, and calls in function main are listed as follows:

```
#include <iostream>
#include <vector>
#include <string>

class Book
{
```

```cpp
private:
    std::string title;
    int pages;
public:
    Book();
    Book(const std::string& atitle, int apages);
    void printdata();
    std::string gettitle() const;
    int getpages() const;
    void settitle(const std::string& atitle);
    void setpages(int apages);
};

Book::Book() : title{ "Default Book Title" }, pages{ 0 }
{
}

Book::Book(const std::string& atitle, int apages) : title{ atitle },
pages{ apages }
{
}

void Book::printdata()
{
    std::cout << "The book title is: " << title << ", and the number of
    pages is: " << pages << '\n';
}

std::string Book::gettitle() const
{
    return title;
}

int Book::getpages() const
{
    return pages;
}
```

```
void Book::settitle(const std::string& atitle)
{
    title = atitle;
}

void Book::setpages(int apages)
{
    pages = apages;
}

int main()
{
    Book defaultbook;
    std::cout << "Default constructor invoked." << '\n';

    Book mybook{ "My Book Title", 123 };
    std::cout << "User-provided constructor invoked." << '\n';
    mybook.printdata();

    std::cout << "The book title is: " << mybook.gettitle() << '\n';
    std::cout << "The number of pages is: " << mybook.getpages() << '\n';

    std::cout << "Setting the new title... " << '\n';
    mybook.settitle("New Book Title");
    std::cout << "Setting the new number of pages... " << '\n';
    mybook.setpages(456);
    mybook.printdata();
}
```

Output:

```
Default constructor invoked.
User-provided constructor invoked.
The book title is: My Book Title, and the number of pages is: 123
The book title is: My Book Title
The number of pages is: 123
```

```
Setting the new title...
Setting the new number of pages...
The book title is: New Book Title, and the number of pages is: 456
```

One final thing left to do is to create a container of objects inside a function main and loop through the container. We will use std::vector<Book> v; to hold, for example, five different objects of type Book. In the vector's initializer list, we will create five temporary objects whose lifetime is bound to a lifetime of a vector. Next, we will iterate through a vector using the range-based for loop and invoke the printdata() member function for each object. For simplicity reasons, we will use the auto& reference type inside the range-based for loop, thus avoiding creating internal copies of objects. Listing:

```cpp
#include <iostream>
#include <vector>
#include <string>

class Book
{
private:
    std::string title;
    int pages;
public:
    Book();
    Book(const std::string& atitle, int apages);
    void printdata();
    std::string gettitle() const;
    int getpages() const;
    void settitle(const std::string& atitle);
    void setpages(int apages);
};

Book::Book() : title{ "Default Book Title" }, pages{ 0 }
{
}

Book::Book(const std::string& atitle, int apages) : title{ atitle },
pages{ apages }
```

```cpp
{
}

void Book::printdata()
{
    std::cout << "The book title is: " << title << ", and the number of
    pages is: " << pages << '\n';
}

std::string Book::gettitle() const
{
    return title;
}

int Book::getpages() const
{
    return pages;
}

void Book::settitle(const std::string& atitle)
{
    title = atitle;
}

void Book::setpages(int apages)
{
    pages = apages;
}

int main()
{
    Book defaultbook;
    std::cout << "Default constructor invoked." << '\n';

    Book mybook{ "My Book Title", 123 };
    std::cout << "User-provided constructor invoked." << '\n';
    mybook.printdata();

    std::cout << "The book title is: " << mybook.gettitle() << '\n';
    std::cout << "The number of pages is: " << mybook.getpages() << '\n';
```

```
    std::cout << "Setting the new title... " << '\n';
    mybook.settitle("New Book Title");
    std::cout << "Setting the new number of pages... " << '\n';
    mybook.setpages(456);
    mybook.printdata();

    std::cout << "\nCreating an inventory of books... " << '\n';
    std::vector<Book> v = {
        Book("Sample Book Title 1", 100),
        Book("Sample Book Title 2", 200),
        Book("Sample Book Title 3", 300),
        Book("Sample Book Title 4", 400),
        Book("Sample Book Title 5", 500),
    };
    for (auto& el : v)
    {
        el.printdata();
    }
}
```

Output:

```
Default constructor invoked.
User-provided constructor invoked.
The book title is: My Book Title, and the number of pages is: 123
The book title is: My Book Title
The number of pages is: 123
Setting the new title...
Setting the new number of pages...
The book title is: New Book Title, and the number of pages is: 456

Creating an inventory of books...
The book title is: Sample Book Title 1, and the number of pages is: 100
The book title is: Sample Book Title 2, and the number of pages is: 200
The book title is: Sample Book Title 3, and the number of pages is: 300
The book title is: Sample Book Title 4, and the number of pages is: 400
The book title is: Sample Book Title 5, and the number of pages is: 500
```

Project II: Book Inventory – Multiple Files

Write a program that splits the code from *Project I* into multiple (source and header) files. Additional requirements:

- Split the code into multiple header and source files.

- Put the class declaration inside a *book.h* header file. Implement header guards.

- Put the class definition inside a *book.cpp* source file. Include the *book.h* header file into a book.cpp source file.

- Put the function `main` inside the *source.cpp* source file. Include the *book.h* header file into a *source.cpp* source file.

- Include additional header files where appropriate.

- Compile all the source files and run the program.

Now, we have three different files, one header file called *book.h* and two source files called *book.cpp* and *source.cpp*.

If you are running Visual Studio, choose *File ➤ New ➤ Project... ➤ Empty Project*, click *Next*, give it a name, and click *Create*. Right-click a project name in the Solution Explorer, choose *Add ➤ New Item...*, choose a *Header File* option, give it the name of *book.h*, and click *Add*. To add a source file, right-click a project name, choose *Add ➤ New Item...*, choose a *Source File* option, give it the name of *book.cpp*, and click *Add*. Repeat the process for a *source.cpp* file.

If you are on Linux or using a different compiler, simply create these three files using the editor of your choice and place them into the same folder. At the end of this project, we will learn how to compile multiple source files using GCC and Visual Studio. Since we have only one class, having only one user-provided header file is sufficient. Now, our basic source code skeleton would look like this:

book.h:

```
#include <iostream>
#include <vector>
#include <string>
```

book.cpp:

```
#include "book.h"
```

source.cpp:

```
#include "book.h"

int main()
{

}
```

For now, the header file only holds several standard library headers we will be using later on. Both source files include the same *book.h* header file. And *source.cpp* holds the function main. This is the basic project layout. Let us expand on this and add the class declaration inside a *book.h* header file. Listing:

book.h:

```
#include <iostream>
#include <vector>
#include <string>

class Book
{
private:
    std::string title;
    int pages;
public:
    Book();
    Book(const std::string& atitle, int apages);
    void printdata();
    std::string gettitle() const;
    int getpages() const;
    void settitle(const std::string& atitle);
    void setpages(int apages);
};
```

We have placed the Book's class declaration inside a *book.h* header file. Let us now implement the header guards for our header file. Listing:

book.h:

```
#ifndef BOOK_H
#define BOOK_H

#include <iostream>
#include <vector>
#include <string>

class Book
{
private:
    std::string title;
    int pages;
public:
    Book();
    Book(const std::string& atitle, int apages);
    void printdata();
    std::string gettitle() const;
    int getpages() const;
    void settitle(const std::string& atitle);
    void setpages(int apages);
};

#endif
```

Now, the entire content of the header file is wrapped inside a header guard. This ensures no multiple inclusions of the same header file will occur during the compilation process, even though we do have multiple inclusions of the same header file in our source files. Let us implement the Book class definition inside a *book.cpp* source file. Listing:

book.cpp:

```
#include "book.h"

Book::Book() : title{ "Default Book Title" }, pages{ 0 }
{
}
```

```cpp
Book::Book(const std::string& atitle, int apages) : title{ atitle },
pages{ apages }
{
}

void Book::printdata()
{
    std::cout << "The book title is: " << title << ", and the number of
    pages is: " << pages << '\n';
}

std::string Book::gettitle() const
{
    return title;
}

int Book::getpages() const
{
    return pages;
}

void Book::settitle(const std::string& atitle)
{
    title = atitle;
}

void Book::setpages(int apages)
{
    pages = apages;
}
```

Finally, let us add the functionality to our main program inside the *source.cpp* file.
Listing:

   source.cpp:

```cpp
#include "book.h"

int main()
{
```

```cpp
    Book defaultbook;
    std::cout << "Default constructor invoked." << '\n';

    Book mybook{ "My Book Title", 123 };
    std::cout << "User-provided constructor invoked." << '\n';
    mybook.printdata();

    std::cout << "The book title is: " << mybook.gettitle() << '\n';
    std::cout << "The number of pages is: " << mybook.getpages() << '\n';

    std::cout << "Setting the new title... " << '\n';
    mybook.settitle("New Book Title");
    std::cout << "Setting the new number of pages... " << '\n';
    mybook.setpages(456);
    mybook.printdata();

    std::cout << "\nCreating an inventory of books... " << '\n';
    std::vector<Book> v = {
        Book("Sample Book Title 1", 100),
        Book("Sample Book Title 2", 200),
        Book("Sample Book Title 3", 300),
        Book("Sample Book Title 4", 400),
        Book("Sample Book Title 5", 500),
    };
    for (auto& el : v)
    {
        el.printdata();
    }
}
```

To rebuild a project in Visual Studio, we press Alt+B+R. To compile and run a program in Visual Studio, press F5 or Ctrl+F5. If we are using GCC, we need to compile all the source files using the following compilation string:

```
g++ -Wall -std=c++17 book.cpp source.cpp
```

And then run the program:

```
./a.out
```

Output:

```
Default constructor invoked.
User-provided constructor invoked.
The book title is: My Book Title, and the number of pages is: 123
The book title is: My Book Title
The number of pages is: 123
Setting the new title...
Setting the new number of pages...
The book title is: New Book Title, and the number of pages is: 456

Creating an inventory of books...
The book title is: Sample Book Title 1, and the number of pages is: 100
The book title is: Sample Book Title 2, and the number of pages is: 200
The book title is: Sample Book Title 3, and the number of pages is: 300
The book title is: Sample Book Title 4, and the number of pages is: 400
The book title is: Sample Book Title 5, and the number of pages is: 500
```

This approach, where we separate our code into multiple header and source files, closely matches the situation we can encounter in real-world scenarios.

Class and even freestanding function declarations are usually placed inside header files, and definitions go inside a separate source file.

The class code can also be wrapped into a namespace, which can be a bonus requirement left to the reader as an exercise.

Project III: Message Logger

Write a program that creates a message logger. The logging functionality will be implemented inside a MyLogger class. The main function creates an instance of a class and logs messages to a console window and a file. Requirements:

- Implement the following methods:

  - void logToFile(...) – A member function that logs a message to a file

  - void logToConsole(...) – A member function that logs a message to a console window

- void logWithLevel(...) – A member function that logs a message using the specific verbosity level

- void logToAll(...) – A member function that logs a message both to a console window and a file

- Implement at least two constructors.

- Disable the copy semantics for the MyLogger class.

- Implement the move semantics for the MyLogger class.

- In function main, create an instance of a MyLogger class and log messages using member functions.

Let us start. For simplicity reasons, we will place all the source code into a single *source.cpp* file. This file will include several headers, it will have a namespace nm, and inside the namespace will be a class. Finally, there is a function main at the end of our source file. Listing:

```cpp
#include <iostream>
#include <string>
#include <fstream>

namespace nm {

    class MyLogger
    {

    };
}

int main()
{

}
```

Let us now add an external constant (outside the class) of type const std::string, called defaultlogfile, that will serve as our default file name. We will also add two class data members, one of type std::fstream called fs, which will represent our internal file stream, and one of type std::string called messagestart, which will represent the beginning of our log message. Listing:

```
#include <iostream>
#include <string>
#include <fstream>

namespace nm {

    const std::string defaultlogfile = "defaultlogfile.txt";

    class MyLogger
    {
    private:
        std::fstream fs;
        std::string messagestart;
    };
}

int main()
{

}
```

Now, we are ready to add one default constructor and a destructor. The default constructor will use the defaultlogfile as a name for our file stream fs. The default constructor will open a file for appending the data, and the destructor will close the file. In our main function, we can now create a single instance of a MyLogger class. Listing:

```
#include <iostream>
#include <string>
#include <fstream>

namespace nm {

    const std::string defaultlogfile = "defaultlogfile.txt";

    class MyLogger
    {
    private:
        std::fstream fs;
        std::string messagestart;
```

369

```
    public:
        MyLogger(); // user-provided default constructor
        ~MyLogger(); // destructor
    };

    // default constructor
    MyLogger::MyLogger()
    {
        fs.open(defaultlogfile, std::ios::app);
        messagestart = "Started logging to a default file. ";
    }

    // destructor
    MyLogger::~MyLogger()
    {
        fs.close(); // close the file
    }

}

int main()
{
    // create an object using the default log file name
    nm::MyLogger o1;
}
```

So far, there is no output on a console window, but a few things happen behind the scenes. In function main, we create an object of a class MyLogger using no parameters, and we name this object o1. This invokes a default constructor MyLogger(), which opens (or creates one if nonexistent) a file with the name *"defaultlogfile.txt"* for appending the data. When the object o1 goes out of scope, the ~MyLogger() destructor gets invoked and closes the file.

Let us now add another user-provided constructor that accepts one parameter of type std::string called customlogfile, which allows us to create an output file with a custom name. In function main, we create another object and provide a custom file name as a parameter. Listing:

```cpp
#include <iostream>
#include <string>
#include <fstream>

namespace nm {

    const std::string defaultlogfile = "defaultlogfile.txt";

    class MyLogger
    {
    private:
        std::fstream fs;
        std::string messagestart;
    public:
        MyLogger(); // user-provided default constructor
        explicit MyLogger(const std::string& customlogfile);
        // user-provided constructor
        ~MyLogger(); // destructor
    };

    // default constructor
    MyLogger::MyLogger()
    {
        fs.open(defaultlogfile, std::ios::app);
        messagestart = "Started logging to a default file. ";
    }

    // user-provided constructor
    MyLogger::MyLogger(const std::string& customlogfile)
    {
        messagestart = " Started logging. ";
        fs.open(customlogfile, std::ios::app); // open the file
    }
```

```
    // destructor
    MyLogger::~MyLogger()
    {
        fs.close(); // close the file
    }

}

int main()
{
    // create an object using the default log file name
    nm::MyLogger o1;

    // create an object using a custom log file name
    nm::MyLogger o2{ "mylogfile.txt" };
}
```

This example creates a second object called o2 and invokes the second user-provided constructor. The second constructor creates another log file called using the name provided as an argument. In our case, it is the *"mylogfile.txt"* file name. Please note that single-argument constructors in C++ should be marked as explicit, thus preventing unwanted constructor conversions by the compiler.

Let us now add two member functions, logToFile() and logToConsole(), for logging the data to a console window and a file, and we will place them above the constructors. Finally, in function main, we will invoke these member functions using both the objects o1 and o2. Listing:

```
#include <iostream>
#include <string>
#include <fstream>

namespace nm {

    const std::string defaultlogfile = "defaultlogfile.txt";

    class MyLogger
    {
    private:
        std::fstream fs;
        std::string messagestart;
```

```
public:
    void logToFile(const std::string& message);
    void logToConsole(const std::string& message);
    MyLogger(); // user-provided default constructor
    explicit MyLogger(const std::string& customlogfile);
    // user-provided constructor
    ~MyLogger(); // destructor
};

void MyLogger::logToFile(const std::string& message)
{
    messagestart = "FILE log: ";
    fs << message << '\n';
}

void MyLogger::logToConsole(const std::string& message)
{
    messagestart = "CONSOLE log: ";
    std::cout << messagestart << message << '\n';
}

// default constructor
MyLogger::MyLogger()
{
    fs.open(defaultlogfile, std::ios::app);
    messagestart = "Started logging to a default file. ";
}

// user-provided constructor
MyLogger::MyLogger(const std::string& customlogfile)
{
    messagestart = " Started logging. ";
    fs.open(customlogfile, std::ios::app); // open the file
}
```

```
    // destructor
    MyLogger::~MyLogger()
    {
        fs.close(); // close the file
    }

}

int main()
{
    // create an object using the default log file name
    nm::MyLogger o1;
    o1.logToConsole("Console log message 1.");
    o1.logToFile("Default file name log message 1.");

    // create an object using a custom log file name
    nm::MyLogger o2{ "mylogfile.txt" };
    o2.logToConsole("Console log message 1.");
    o2.logToFile("Custom file name log message 1.");
}
```

Output:

```
CONSOLE log: Console log message 1.
CONSOLE log: Console log message 1.
```

The logToConsole() and logToFile() member functions modify the value of a messagestart field and log the argument's value to appropriate destinations. The content of the *"defaultlogfile.txt"* file is

File Output:

```
Default file name log message 1.
```

And the content of the *"mylogfile.txt"* file is

File Output:

```
Custom file name log message 1.
```

Let us now add the member function called `logWithLevel` that accepts two arguments, a message to be logged and a message verbosity level. Let us say there are three verbosity levels: `LOG_INFO`, `LOG_WARNING`, and `LOG_ALL`. The message verbosity levels can be represented by an enum we place above our class. We will then use this enum as a type for the function's second parameter. Finally, we invoke the function for both objects. Listing:

```cpp
#include <iostream>
#include <string>
#include <fstream>

namespace nm {
    // different logging verbosity levels
    enum class LoggingLevels
    {
        LOG_INFO,
        LOG_WARNING,
        LOG_ALL
    };

    const std::string defaultlogfile = "defaultlogfile.txt";

    class MyLogger
    {
    private:
        std::fstream fs;
        std::string messagestart;
    public:
        void logToFile(const std::string& message);
        void logToConsole(const std::string& message);
        void logWithLevel(const std::string& message, LoggingLevels
        loglevel);

        MyLogger(); // user-provided default constructor
        explicit MyLogger(const std::string& customlogfile);
        // user-provided constructor
```

```
    ~MyLogger(); // destructor
};

void MyLogger::logToFile(const std::string& message)
{
    messagestart = "FILE log: ";
    fs << message << '\n';
}

void MyLogger::logToConsole(const std::string& message)
{
    messagestart = "CONSOLE log: ";
    std::cout << messagestart << message << '\n';
}

void MyLogger::logWithLevel(const std::string& message, LoggingLevels
loglevel)
{
    switch (loglevel)
    {
    case LoggingLevels::LOG_INFO:
        logToConsole("Log level INFO: " + message);
        break;
    case LoggingLevels::LOG_WARNING:
        logToConsole("Log level WARNING: " + message);
        break;
    case LoggingLevels::LOG_ALL:
        logToConsole("Log level ALL: " + message);
        break;
    default:
        logToConsole("No logging level: " + message);
        break;
    }
}

// default constructor
MyLogger::MyLogger()
```

```
    {
        fs.open(defaultlogfile, std::ios::app);
        messagestart = "Started logging to a default file. ";
    }

    // user-provided constructor
    MyLogger::MyLogger(const std::string& customlogfile) {
        messagestart = " Started logging. ";
        fs.open(customlogfile, std::ios::app); // open the file
    }

    // destructor
    MyLogger::~MyLogger()
    {
        fs.close(); // close the file
    }
}

int main()
{
    // create an object using the default log file name
    nm::MyLogger o1;
    o1.logToConsole("Console log message 1.");
    o1.logToFile("Default file name log message 1.");
    o1.logWithLevel("Console log message 2.", nm::LoggingLevels::LOG_INFO);

    // create an object using a custom log file name
    nm::MyLogger o2{ "mylogfile.txt" };
    o2.logToConsole("Console log message 1.");
    o2.logToFile("Custom file name log message 1.");
    o2.logWithLevel("Console log message 3.", nm::LoggingLevels::LOG_
    WARNING);
}
```

Output:

```
CONSOLE log: Console log message 1.
CONSOLE log: Log level INFO: Console log message 2.
CONSOLE log: Console log message 1.
CONSOLE log: Log level WARNING: Console log message 3.
```

In this example, we have added an enum type outside the class. The enum represents three possible levels of logging verbosity. We pass this enum as a second argument to our logWithLevel function and opt for one of three choices. The function uses this enum in a switch statement to update the logging message accordingly. Finally, in function main, we invoke this function using both objects.

Let us now add the logToAll member function that logs both to the console and a file. We will invoke this function in the main program using both objects. Listing:

```cpp
#include <iostream>
#include <string>
#include <fstream>

namespace nm {
    // different logging verbosity levels
    enum class LoggingLevels
    {
        LOG_INFO,
        LOG_WARNING,
        LOG_ALL
    };

    const std::string defaultlogfile = "defaultlogfile.txt";

    class MyLogger
    {
    private:
        std::fstream fs;
        std::string messagestart;
```

```cpp
public:
    void logToFile(const std::string& message);
    void logToConsole(const std::string& message);
    void logWithLevel(const std::string& message, LoggingLevels
    loglevel);
    void logToAll(const std::string& message);

    MyLogger(); // user-provided default constructor
    explicit MyLogger(const std::string& customlogfile);
    // user-provided constructor
    ~MyLogger(); // destructor
};

void MyLogger::logToFile(const std::string& message)
{
    messagestart = "FILE log: ";
    fs << message << '\n';
}

void MyLogger::logToConsole(const std::string& message)
{
    messagestart = "CONSOLE log: ";
    std::cout << messagestart << message << '\n';
}

void MyLogger::logWithLevel(const std::string& message, LoggingLevels
loglevel)
{
    switch (loglevel)
    {
    case LoggingLevels::LOG_INFO:
        logToConsole("Log level INFO: " + message);
        break;
    case LoggingLevels::LOG_WARNING:
        logToConsole("Log level WARNING: " + message);
        break;
    case LoggingLevels::LOG_ALL:
```

```cpp
                logToConsole("Log level ALL: " + message);
                break;
            default:
                logToConsole("No logging level: " + message);
                break;
        }
    }

    void MyLogger::logToAll(const std::string& message)
    {
        logToConsole(message);
        logToFile(message);
    }

    // default constructor
    MyLogger::MyLogger()
    {
        fs.open(defaultlogfile, std::ios::app);
        messagestart = "Started logging to a default file. ";
    }

    // user-provided constructor
    MyLogger::MyLogger(const std::string& customlogfile) {
        messagestart = " Started logging. ";
        fs.open(customlogfile, std::ios::app); // open the file
    }

    // destructor
    MyLogger::~MyLogger()
    {
        fs.close(); // close the file
    }
}

int main()
{
```

```
// create an object using the default log file name
nm::MyLogger o1;

o1.logToConsole("Console log message 1.");
o1.logToFile("Default file name log message 1.");
o1.logWithLevel("Console log message 2.", nm::LoggingLevels::LOG_INFO);
o1.logToAll("Logging to both the console and a file from o1.");
// create an object using a custom log file name
nm::MyLogger o2{ "mylogfile.txt" };
o2.logToConsole("Console log message 1.");
o2.logToFile("Custom file name log message 1.");
o2.logWithLevel("Console log message 3.", nm::LoggingLevels::LOG_
WARNING);
o2.logToAll("Logging to both the console and a file from o2.");
}
```

Output:

```
CONSOLE log: Console log message 1.
CONSOLE log: Log level INFO: Console log message 2.
CONSOLE log: Logging to both the console and a file from o1.
CONSOLE log: Console log message 1.
CONSOLE log: Log level WARNING: Console log message 3.
CONSOLE log: Logging to both the console and a file from o2.
```

We have implemented and called the logToAll member function that logs the message to a console window and a file. It does so by internally calling the logToConsole and logToFile functions, thus reusing the existing code and saving us from having to retype the code by hand.

The std::fstream is not copiable, it is only movable, so it makes sense that our class should not be copiable. It should be movable. Let us disable the copy semantics for our class (copy constructor and copy assignment operator) and implement the move constructor and move assignment operator. In function main, we will create the third object called o3 by moving the data from o2 to o3. Listing:

```cpp
#include <iostream>
#include <string>
#include <fstream>

namespace nm {
    // different logging verbosity levels
    enum class LoggingLevels
    {
        LOG_INFO,
        LOG_WARNING,
        LOG_ALL
    };

    const std::string defaultlogfile = "defaultlogfile.txt";

    class MyLogger
    {
    private:
        std::fstream fs;
        std::string messagestart;
    public:
        void logToFile(const std::string& message);
        void logToConsole(const std::string& message);
        void logWithLevel(const std::string& message, LoggingLevels
        loglevel);
        void logToAll(const std::string& message);

        MyLogger(); // user-provided default constructor
        explicit MyLogger(const std::string& customlogfile); // user-
        provided constructor
        MyLogger(const MyLogger& rhs) = delete; // disable the copy
        constructor
        MyLogger& operator=(const MyLogger& rhs) = delete; // disable the
        copy assignment operator
        MyLogger(MyLogger&& rhs) noexcept; // move constructor
        MyLogger& operator=(MyLogger&& rhs) noexcept; // move assignment
        operator
```

```cpp
    ~MyLogger(); // destructor
};

void MyLogger::logToFile(const std::string& message)
{
    messagestart = "FILE log: ";
    fs << message << '\n';
}

void MyLogger::logToConsole(const std::string& message)
{
    messagestart = "CONSOLE log: ";
    std::cout << messagestart << message << '\n';
}

void MyLogger::logWithLevel(const std::string& message, LoggingLevels
loglevel)
{
    switch (loglevel)
    {
    case LoggingLevels::LOG_INFO:
        logToConsole("Log level INFO: " + message);
        break;
    case LoggingLevels::LOG_WARNING:
        logToConsole("Log level WARNING: " + message);
        break;
    case LoggingLevels::LOG_ALL:
        logToConsole("Log level ALL: " + message);
        break;
    default:
        logToConsole("No logging level: " + message);
        break;
    }
}

void MyLogger::logToAll(const std::string& message)
{
```

```
        logToConsole(message);
        logToFile(message);
    }

    // default constructor
    MyLogger::MyLogger()
    {
        fs.open(defaultlogfile, std::ios::app);
        messagestart = "Started logging to a default file. ";
    }

    // user-provided constructor
    MyLogger::MyLogger(const std::string& customlogfile) {
        messagestart = " Started logging. ";
        fs.open(customlogfile, std::ios::app); // open the file
    }

    // move constructor
    MyLogger::MyLogger(MyLogger&& rhs) noexcept
        :fs{ std::move(rhs.fs) }, messagestart{ rhs.messagestart }
    {
    }

    // move assignment operator
    MyLogger& MyLogger::operator=(MyLogger&& rhs) noexcept
    {
        messagestart = std::move(rhs.messagestart);
        fs = std::move(rhs.fs);
        return *this;
    }

    // destructor
    MyLogger::~MyLogger()
    {
        fs.close(); // close the file
    }
}
```

```
int main()
{
    // create an object using the default log file name
    nm::MyLogger o1;
    o1.logToConsole("Console log message 1.");
    o1.logToFile("Default file name log message 1.");
    o1.logWithLevel("Console log message 2.", nm::LoggingLevels::LOG_INFO);
    o1.logToAll("Logging to both the console and a file from o1.");

    // create an object using a custom log file name
    nm::MyLogger o2{ "mylogfile.txt" };
    o2.logToConsole("Console log message 1.");
    o2.logToFile("Custom file name log message 1.");
    o2.logWithLevel("Console log message 3.", nm::LoggingLevels::
    LOG_WARNING);
    o2.logToAll("Logging to both the console and a file from o2.");
    // create an object using a move operation
    nm::MyLogger o3 = std::move(o2);
    o3.logToAll("Logging to both the console and a file from o3.");
}
```

Output:

```
CONSOLE log: Console log message 1.
CONSOLE log: Log level INFO: Console log message 2.
CONSOLE log: Logging to both the console and a file from o1.
CONSOLE log: Console log message 1.
CONSOLE log: Log level WARNING: Console log message 3.
CONSOLE log: Logging to both the console and a file from o2.
CONSOLE log: Logging to both the console and a file from o3.
```

We have disabled the copy semantics by using the = delete; syntax in the declaration of a copy constructor and copy assignment. We then implemented the move constructor and move assignment operator. Finally, in our main function, we created a third object named o3 by moving data from object o2. Finally, we invoke the logToAll member function for the third object. Our project is now complete.

Project IV: Message Logger – Multiple Files

Write a program that splits the code from *Project III* into multiple (source and header) files. Additional requirements:

- Split the code into multiple header and source files.

- Put the MyLogger class declaration inside a *mylogger.h* header file. Implement header guards.

- Put the enum and a constant inside a *mylogger.h* header file. Implement header guards.

- Put the MyLogger class definition inside a *mylogger.cpp* source file. Include the *mylogger.h* header file into a *mylogger*.cpp source file.

- Put the function main inside the *source.cpp* source file. Include the *mylogger.h* header file into a *source.cpp* source file.

- Include additional header files where appropriate.

- Wrap the code inside *mylogger.h* and *mylogger.cpp* into a namespace nm.

- Compile all the source files and run the program.

Now, we have three different files, one header file called *mylogger.h* and two source files called *mylogger.cpp* and *source.cpp*. The basic, almost empty project skeleton now looks like this:

mylogger.h:

```
#include <iostream>
#include <string>
#include <fstream>
```

mylogger.cpp:

```
#include "mylogger.h"
```

source.cpp:

```
#include "mylogger.h"

int main()
```

386

```
{

}
```

First, let us add a header guard to our *mylogger.h* header file. Listing: *mylogger.h*:

```
#ifndef MYLOGGER_H
#define MYLOGGER_H

#include <iostream>
#include <string>
#include <fstream>

#endif // !MYLOGGER_H
```

Let us now add the nm namespace to both the *mylogger.h* header file and the *mylogger.cpp* source file. Listing:

mylogger.h:

```
#ifndef MYLOGGER_H
#define MYLOGGER_H

#include <iostream>
#include <string>
#include <fstream>

namespace nm
{

}

#endif // !MYLOGGER_H
```

mylogger.cpp:

```
#include "mylogger.h"

namespace nm
{

}
```

Inside the *mylogger.h* header file, we will add the enum type declaration, a constant for a file name, and a class declaration. And we will place that code inside the nm namespace. Listing:

mylogger.h:

```
#ifndef MYLOGGER_H
#define MYLOGGER_H

#include <iostream>
#include <string>
#include <fstream>

namespace nm
{
    // different logging verbosity levels
    enum class LoggingLevels
    {
        LOG_INFO,
        LOG_WARNING,
        LOG_ALL
    };

    const std::string defaultlogfile = "defaultlogfile.txt";

    class MyLogger
    {
    private:
        std::fstream fs;
        std::string messagestart;
    public:
        void logToFile(const std::string& message);
        void logToConsole(const std::string& message);
        void logWithLevel(const std::string& message, LoggingLevels
        loglevel);
        void logToAll(const std::string& message);

        MyLogger(); // user-provided default constructor
```

```
    explicit MyLogger(const std::string& customlogfile); // user-
    provided constructor
    MyLogger(const MyLogger& rhs) = delete; // disable the copy
    constructor
    MyLogger& operator=(const MyLogger& rhs) = delete; // disable the
    copy assignment operator
    MyLogger(MyLogger&& rhs) noexcept; // move constructor
    MyLogger& operator=(MyLogger&& rhs) noexcept; // move assignment
    operator
    ~MyLogger(); // destructor
    };
}

#endif // !MYLOGGER_H
```

Let us now add the MyLogger class definition to our *mylogger.cpp* source file. We will place the definition inside the nm namespace. Listing:

mylogger.cpp:

```
#include "mylogger.h"

namespace nm
{
    void MyLogger::logToFile(const std::string& message)
    {
        messagestart = "FILE log: ";
        fs << message << '\n';
    }

    void MyLogger::logToConsole(const std::string& message)
    {
        messagestart = "CONSOLE log: ";
        std::cout << messagestart << message << '\n';
    }
```

```cpp
void MyLogger::logWithLevel(const std::string& message, LoggingLevels
loglevel)
{
    switch (loglevel)
    {
    case LoggingLevels::LOG_INFO:
        logToConsole("Log level INFO: " + message);
        break;
    case LoggingLevels::LOG_WARNING:
        logToConsole("Log level WARNING: " + message);
        break;
    case LoggingLevels::LOG_ALL:
        logToConsole("Log level ALL: " + message);
        break;
    default:
        logToConsole("No logging level: " + message);
        break;
    }
}

void MyLogger::logToAll(const std::string& message)
{
    logToConsole(message);
    logToFile(message);
}

// default constructor
MyLogger::MyLogger()
{
    fs.open(defaultlogfile, std::ios::app);
    messagestart = "Started logging to a default file. ";
}

// user-provided constructor
MyLogger::MyLogger(const std::string& customlogfile) {
    messagestart = " Started logging. ";
    fs.open(customlogfile, std::ios::app); // open the file
}
```

```cpp
    // move constructor
    MyLogger::MyLogger(MyLogger&& rhs) noexcept
        :fs{ std::move(rhs.fs) }, messagestart{ rhs.messagestart }
    {
    }

    // move assignment operator
    MyLogger& MyLogger::operator=(MyLogger&& rhs) noexcept
    {
        messagestart = std::move(rhs.messagestart);
        fs = std::move(rhs.fs);
        return *this;
    }

    // destructor
    MyLogger::~MyLogger()
    {
        fs.close(); // close the file
    }
}
```

One final thing left to do is to add the functionality to our function main inside the *source.cpp* source file. Listing:

source.cpp:

```cpp
#include "mylogger.h"

int main()
{
    // create an object using the default log file name
    nm::MyLogger o1;
    o1.logToConsole("Console log message 1.");
    o1.logToFile("Default file name log message 1.");
    o1.logWithLevel("Console log message 2.", nm::LoggingLevels::LOG_INFO);
    o1.logToAll("Logging to both the console and a file from o1.");

    // create an object using a custom log file name
    nm::MyLogger o2{ "mylogfile.txt" };
```

```
o2.logToConsole("Console log message 1.");
o2.logToFile("Custom file name log message 1.");
o2.logWithLevel("Console log message 3.", nm::LoggingLevels::LOG_
WARNING);
o2.logToAll("Logging to both the console and a file from o2.");

// create an object using a move operation
nm::MyLogger o3 = std::move(o2);
o3.logToAll("Logging to both the console and a file from o3.");
}
```

Output:

```
CONSOLE log: Console log message 1.
CONSOLE log: Log level INFO: Console log message 2.
CONSOLE log: Logging to both the console and a file from o1.
CONSOLE log: Console log message 1.
CONSOLE log: Log level WARNING: Console log message 3.
CONSOLE log: Logging to both the console and a file from o2.
CONSOLE log: Logging to both the console and a file from o3.
```

Now our project source code is broken up into multiple header and source files. We keep the declarations inside the *mylogger.h* header file, and we keep the class definitions inside the *mylogger.cpp* file. Our main program is located inside the *source.cpp* file. We include the *mylogger.h* header in both source files and compile and run our program. We should get into a good habit of separating declarations and definitions to multiple header and source files. This concludes the Project IV requirements.

Project V: Information System

Write a program that represents an employee's information system. The system is implemented as a container of polymorphic objects. Requirements:

- Create a base class called `Person`, having multiple constructors and at least one virtual member function.

- Create a derived class called `Employee`, extending the `Person`'s functionality. The `Employee` class overrides the virtual member function from the base class.

- Wrap the classes into a namespace.

- Both classes support the copy and move semantics.

- In function `main`, create a container of multiple polymorphic objects (pointers). Iterate through a container and invoke at least one member function.

Let us get started. We will place the entire source code inside a single *source.cpp* source file. Our project skeleton looks like this:

```cpp
#include <iostream>
#include <string>
#include <vector>
#include <memory>

namespace nm
{

}

using namespace nm;

int main()
{

}
```

So far, we have included several standard library headers we will be using, we created an empty nm namespace in the global region of a source file, we then introduced the entire namespace to the current scope, and, finally, we have a function `main`.

Let us now add the two classes' declarations inside the nm namespace. Listing:

```cpp
#include <iostream>
#include <string>
#include <vector>
```

```
#include <memory>

namespace nm
{
    // base class Person
    class Person
    {

    };

    // derived class Employee
    class Employee : public Person
    {

    };
}

using namespace nm;

int main()
{

}
```

Now, we will focus on the first class, Person. Let us add a couple of fields to our base class Person. Listing:

```
#include <iostream>
#include <string>
#include <vector>
#include <memory>
namespace nm
{
    // base class Person
    class Person
    {
    private:
        std::string name;
        int age;
    };
```

```
    // derived class Employee
    class Employee : public Person
    {

    };
}

using namespace nm;

int main()
{

}
```

Next, we will add two constructors – one default constructor with no parameters and one with two parameters. We will declare them inside the class body and define them outside the class body. Listing:

```
#include <iostream>
#include <string>
#include <vector>
#include <memory>

namespace nm
{
    // base class Person
    class Person
    {
    private:
        std::string name;
        int age;
    public:
        // default constructor
        Person();
        // user-provided constructor
        Person(const std::string& aname, int argage);
    };
```

```
    Person::Person() : name{ "Default name" }, age{ -1 }
    {
    }

    Person::Person(const std::string& aname, int argage) : name{ aname },
    age{ argage }
    {
    }

    // derived class Employee
    class Employee : public Person
    {

    };
}

using namespace nm;

int main()
{

}
```

The default constructor initializes an object by setting the data member's values to some default values of *Default name* and *-1*. The user-provided constructor, on the other hand, has two parameters and uses them to initialize data members: name and age. It uses its initializer list to perform the initialization operation.

Next, we will add a couple of member functions for printing out the values of name and age data members. Listing:

```
#include <iostream>
#include <string>
#include <vector>
#include <memory>

namespace nm
{
    // base class Person
    class Person
    {
```

```cpp
private:
    std::string name;
    int age;
public:
    // default constructor
    Person();
    // user-provided constructor
    Person(const std::string& aname, int argage);
    void printname();
    void printage();
    void printdata();
};

Person::Person() : name{ "Default name" }, age{ -1 }
{
}

erson::Person(const std::string& aname, int argage) : name{ aname },
age{ argage }
{
}

void Person::printname()
{
    std::cout << name << '\n';
}

void Person::printage()
{
    std::cout << age << '\n';
}

void Person::printdata()
{
    std::cout << name << ' ' << age << '\n';
}
```

```
    // derived class Employee
    class Employee : public Person
    {

    };
}

using namespace nm;

int main()
{

}
```

Next, we will add getters and setters for both the name and age fields. In total, we will add four member functions. Getters should be marked as const as they promise not to change any data members' values. Listing:

```
#include <iostream>
#include <string>
#include <vector>
#include <memory>

namespace nm
{
    // base class Person
    class Person
    {
    private:
        std::string name;
        int age;
    public:
        // default constructor
        Person();
        // user-provided constructor
        Person(const std::string& aname, int argage);
        void printname();
        void printage();
        void printdata();
```

```cpp
    std::string getname() const;
    int getage() const;
    void setname(const std::string& aname);
    void setage(int argage);
};

Person::Person() : name{ "Default name" }, age{ -1 }
{
}

Person::Person(const std::string& aname, int argage) : name{ aname },
age{ argage }
{
}

void Person::printname()
{
    std::cout << name << '\n';
}

void Person::printage()
{
    std::cout << age << '\n';
}

void Person::printdata()
{
    std::cout << name << ' ' << age << '\n';
}

std::string Person::getname() const
{
    return name;
}

int Person::getage() const
{
    return age;
}
```

```cpp
void Person::setname(const std::string& aname)
{
    name = aname;
}

void Person::setage(int argage)
{
    age = argage;
}

// derived class Employee
class Employee : public Person
{

};
}

using namespace nm;


int main()
{

}
```

Next, we will add a `virtual` member function `formatprint` that prints the Person's data in a more readable way. We will also add a `virtual` empty destructor to our `Person` class, ensuring the proper destruction of polymorphic objects. Listing:

```cpp
#include <iostream>
#include <string>
#include <vector>
#include <memory>

namespace nm
{
    // base class Person
    class Person
    {
```

```
private:
    std::string name;
    int age;
public:
    // default constructor
    Person();
    // user-provided constructor
    Person(const std::string& aname, int argage);
    void printname();
    void printage();
    void printdata();
    std::string getname() const;
    int getage() const;
    void setname(const std::string& aname);
    void setage(int argage);
    virtual void formatprint();
    // virtual base class destructor
    virtual ~Person() {}
};

Person::Person() : name{ "Default name" }, age{ -1 }
{
}

Person::Person(const std::string& aname, int argage) : name{ aname },
age{ argage }
{
}

void Person::printname()
{
    std::cout << name << '\n';
}

void Person::printage()
{
    std::cout << age << '\n';
}
```

```cpp
void Person::printdata()
{
    std::cout << name << ' ' << age << '\n';
}

std::string Person::getname() const
{
    return name;
}

int Person::getage() const
{
    return age;
}

void Person::setname(const std::string& aname)
{
    name = aname;
}

void Person::setage(int argage)
{
    age = argage;
}
void Person::formatprint()
{
    std::cout << "Person's name: " << name << ", age: " << age << '\n';
}

// derived class Employee
class Employee : public Person
{

};
}
```

```
using namespace nm;

int main()
{

}
```

One final thing left to do is to add the copy and move constructors and assignment operators to our Person class. We will place those functions below our existing constructors. Listing:

```
#include <iostream>
#include <string>
#include <vector>
#include <memory>

namespace nm
{
    // base class Person
    class Person
    {
    private:
        std::string name;
        int age;
    public:
        // default constructor
        Person();
        // user-provided constructor
        Person(const std::string& aname, int argage);
        // copy constructor
        Person(const Person& rhs);
        // copy assignment operator
        Person& operator=(const Person& rhs);
        // move constructor
        Person(Person&& rhs) noexcept;
        // move assignment operator
        Person& operator=(Person&& rhs) noexcept;
        void printname();
```

```cpp
        void printage();
        void printdata();
        std::string getname() const;
        int getage() const;
        void setname(const std::string& aname);
        void setage(int argage);
        virtual void formatprint();
        // virtual base class destructor
        virtual ~Person() {}
};

Person::Person() : name{ "Default name" }, age{ -1 }
{
}

Person::Person(const std::string& aname, int argage) : name{ aname },
age{ argage }
{
}

Person::Person(const Person& rhs) : name{ rhs.name }, age{ rhs.age }
{
}

Person& Person::operator=(const Person& rhs)
{
    name = rhs.name;
    age = rhs.age;
    return *this;
}

Person::Person(Person&& rhs) noexcept : name{ std::move(rhs.name) },
 age{ std::move(rhs.age) }
{
}

Person& Person::operator=(Person&& rhs) noexcept
{
```

```cpp
    name = std::move(name);
    age = std::move(age);
    return *this;
}
void Person::printname()
{
    std::cout << name << '\n';
}

void Person::printage()
{
    std::cout << age << '\n';
}

void Person::printdata()
{
    std::cout << name << ' ' << age << '\n';
}

std::string Person::getname() const
{
    return name;
}

int Person::getage() const
{
    return age;
}

void Person::setname(const std::string& aname)
{
    name = aname;
}

void Person::setage(int argage)
{
    age = argage;
}
```

```cpp
    void Person::formatprint()
    {
        std::cout << "Person's name: " << name << ", age: " << age << '\n';
    }

    // derived class Employee
    class Employee : public Person
    {

    };
}

using namespace nm;

int main()
{

}
```

We have now completed the Person class functionality. Please note that our move constructor and move assignment operator are marked as noexcept, thus making a strong exception guarantee and promising not to raise an exception while executing.

Next, we will extend the derived class Employee. We will add one additional member field called jobtitle. We will also add two constructors, the default one and a user-provided one. Listing:

```cpp
#include <iostream>
#include <string>
#include <vector>
#include <memory>

namespace nm
{
    // base class Person
    class Person
    {
    private:
        std::string name;
        int age;
```

```cpp
public:
    // default constructor
    Person();
    // user-provided constructor
    Person(const std::string& aname, int argage);
    // copy constructor
    Person(const Person& rhs);
    // copy assignment operator
    Person& operator=(const Person& rhs);
    // move constructor
    Person(Person&& rhs) noexcept;
    // move assignment operator
    Person& operator=(Person&& rhs) noexcept;
    void printname();
    void printage();
    void printdata();
    std::string getname() const;
    int getage() const;
    void setname(const std::string& aname);
    void setage(int argage);
    virtual void formatprint();
    // virtual base class destructor
    virtual ~Person() {}
};

Person::Person() : name{ "Default name" }, age{ -1 }
{
}

Person::Person(const std::string& aname, int argage) : name{ aname },
age{ argage }
{
}

Person::Person(const Person& rhs) : name{ rhs.name }, age{ rhs.age }
{
}
```

```cpp
Person& Person::operator=(const Person& rhs)
{
    name = rhs.name;
    age = rhs.age;
    return *this;
}

Person::Person(Person&& rhs) noexcept : name{ std::move(rhs.name) },
age{ std::move(rhs.age) }
{
}

Person& Person::operator=(Person&& rhs) noexcept
{
    name = std::move(name);
    age = std::move(age);
    return *this;
}

void Person::printname()
{
    std::cout << name << '\n';
}

void Person::printage()
{
    std::cout << age << '\n';
}

void Person::printdata()
{
    std::cout << name << ' ' << age << '\n';
}

std::string Person::getname() const
{
    return name;
}
```

```cpp
int Person::getage() const
{
    return age;
}

void Person::setname(const std::string& aname)
{
    name = aname;
}

void Person::setage(int argage)
{
    age = argage;
}

void Person::formatprint()
{
    std::cout << "Person's name: " << name << ", age: " << age << '\n';
}

// derived class Employee
class Employee : public Person
{
private:
    std::string jobtitle;
public:
    // default constructor
    Employee();
    // user provided constructor
    Employee(const std::string& aname, int argage, const std::string&
    ajobtitle);
};

Employee::Employee() : Person(), jobtitle{ "The Default Role" }
{}
```

```
    Employee::Employee(const std::string& aname, int argage, const
    std::string& ajobtitle) : Person(aname, argage), jobtitle{ ajobtitle }
    {}

}

using namespace nm;

int main()
{

}
```

In this iteration, we have added an additional field jobtitle and two constructors to our derived class Employee. The default Employee() constructor calls a base class Person() default constructor in its initializer list to initialize the base class part. Then it proceeds to initialize the jobtitle data member.

Similarly, the second, user-provided Employee(parameters) constructor uses a base class Person(parameters) user-provided constructor to initialize the base class part using its arguments. Then, it proceeds to initialize the remaining jobtitle field.

Let us now complete our Employee class by

- Implementing the copy and move semantics

- Adding getters and setters

- Overriding the formatprint function

Listing:

```
#include <iostream>
#include <string>
#include <vector>
#include <memory>

namespace nm
{
    // base class Person
    class Person
    {
```

```cpp
private:
    std::string name;
    int age;
public:
    // default constructor
    Person();
    // user-provided constructor
    Person(const std::string& aname, int argage);
    // copy constructor
    Person(const Person& rhs);
    // copy assignment operator
    Person& operator=(const Person& rhs);
    // move constructor
    Person(Person&& rhs) noexcept;
    // move assignment operator
    Person& operator=(Person&& rhs) noexcept;
    void printname();
    void printage();
    void printdata();
    std::string getname() const;
    int getage() const;
    void setname(const std::string& aname);
    void setage(int argage);
    virtual void formatprint();
    // virtual base class destructor
    virtual ~Person() {}
};

Person::Person() : name{ "Default name" }, age{ -1 }
{
}

Person::Person(const std::string& aname, int argage) : name{ aname },
age{ argage }
{
}
```

```cpp
Person::Person(const Person& rhs) : name{ rhs.name }, age{ rhs.age }
{
}

Person& Person::operator=(const Person& rhs)
{
    name = rhs.name;
    age = rhs.age;
    return *this;
}

Person::Person(Person&& rhs) noexcept : name{ std::move(rhs.name) },
age{ std::move(rhs.age) }
{
}

Person& Person::operator=(Person&& rhs) noexcept
{
    name = std::move(name);
    age = std::move(age);
    return *this;
}

void Person::printname()
{
    std::cout << name << '\n';
}

void Person::printage()
{
    std::cout << age << '\n';
}
void Person::printdata()
{
    std::cout << name << ' ' << age << '\n';
}

std::string Person::getname() const
```

```cpp
{
    return name;
}

int Person::getage() const
{
    return age;
}

void Person::setname(const std::string& aname)
{
    name = aname;
}

void Person::setage(int argage)
{
    age = argage;
}

void Person::formatprint()
{
    std::cout << "Person's name: " << name << ", age: " << age << '\n';
}

// derived class Employee
class Employee : public Person
{
private:
    std::string jobtitle;
public:
    // default constructor
    Employee();
    // user provided constructor
    Employee(const std::string& aname, int argage, const std::string&
    ajobtitle);
    // copy constructor
    Employee(const Employee& rhs);
    // copy assignment operator
```

```
    Employee& operator=(const Employee& rhs);
    // move constructor
    Employee(Employee&& rhs) noexcept;
    // move assignment operator
    Employee& operator=(Employee&& rhs) noexcept;
    void setjobtitle(const std::string& ajobtitle);
    std::string getjobtitle() const;
    void formatprint() override;
};

Employee::Employee() : Person(), jobtitle{ "The Default Role" }
{}

Employee::Employee(const std::string& aname, int argage, const
std::string& ajobtitle) : Person(aname, argage), jobtitle{ ajobtitle }
{}

Employee::Employee(const Employee& rhs) : Person(rhs), jobtitle{ rhs.
jobtitle }
{
}

Employee& Employee::operator=(const Employee& rhs)
{
    Person::operator=(rhs);
    jobtitle = rhs.jobtitle;
    return *this;
}

Employee::Employee(Employee&& rhs) noexcept : Person(std::move(rhs)),
jobtitle{ std::move(rhs.jobtitle) }
{
}

Employee& Employee::operator=(Employee&& rhs) noexcept
{
    Person::operator=(std::move(rhs));
    jobtitle = std::move(rhs.jobtitle);
```

```
        return *this;
    }

    void Employee::setjobtitle(const std::string& ajobtitle)
    {
        jobtitle = ajobtitle;
    }

    std::string Employee::getjobtitle() const
    {
        return jobtitle;
    }

    void Employee::formatprint()
    {
        std::cout << "Employee's name: " << getname() << ", age: " <<
        getage() << ", job title: " << jobtitle << '\n';
    }
}

using namespace nm;

int main()
{

}
```

The copy and move constructors of a derived class in their initializer lists utilize the copy constructors from a base class to initialize the base class parts.

The copy and move assignment operators of a derived class utilize a base class's copy and move assignment operators to assign the base class parts of the class.

Finally, we override the behavior of the virtual formatprint() function and give it new functionality. One last thing left to do is to create a vector of unique pointers inside a function main and iterate through the container. Listing:

```
#include <iostream>
#include <string>
#include <vector>
#include <memory>
```

```cpp
namespace nm
{
    // base class Person
    class Person
    {
    private:
        std::string name;
        int age;
    public:
        // default constructor
        Person();
        // user-provided constructor
        Person(const std::string& aname, int argage);
        // copy constructor
        Person(const Person& rhs);
        // copy assignment operator
        Person& operator=(const Person& rhs);
        // move constructor
        Person(Person&& rhs) noexcept;
        // move assignment operator
        Person& operator=(Person&& rhs) noexcept;
        void printname();
        void printage();
        void printdata();
        std::string getname() const;
        int getage() const;
        void setname(const std::string& aname);
        void setage(int argage);
        virtual void formatprint();
        // virtual base class destructor
        virtual ~Person() {}
    };

    Person::Person() : name{ "Default name" }, age{ -1 }
    {
    }
```

```cpp
Person::Person(const std::string& aname, int argage) : name{ aname },
age{ argage }
{
}

Person::Person(const Person& rhs) : name{ rhs.name }, age{ rhs.age }
{
}

Person& Person::operator=(const Person& rhs)
{
    name = rhs.name;
    age = rhs.age;
    return *this;
}

Person::Person(Person&& rhs) noexcept : name{ std::move(rhs.name) },
age{ std::move(rhs.age) }
{
}

Person& Person::operator=(Person&& rhs) noexcept
{
    name = std::move(name);
    age = std::move(age);
    return *this;
}

void Person::printname()
{
    std::cout << name << '\n';
}

void Person::printage()
{
    std::cout << age << '\n';
}
```

417

```cpp
void Person::printdata()
{
    std::cout << name << ' ' << age << '\n';
}

std::string Person::getname() const
{
    return name;
}

int Person::getage() const
{
    return age;
}

void Person::setname(const std::string& aname)
{
    name = aname;
}

void Person::setage(int argage)
{
    age = argage;
}

void Person::formatprint()
{
    std::cout << "Person's name: " << name << ", age: " << age << '\n';
}

// derived class Employee
class Employee : public Person
{
private:
    std::string jobtitle;
public:
    // default constructor
    Employee();
```

```cpp
    // user provided constructor
    Employee(const std::string& aname, int argage, const std::string&
    ajobtitle);
    // copy constructor
    Employee(const Employee& rhs);
    // copy assignment operator
    Employee& operator=(const Employee& rhs);
    // move constructor
    Employee(Employee&& rhs) noexcept;
    // move assignment operator
    Employee& operator=(Employee&& rhs) noexcept;
    void setjobtitle(const std::string& ajobtitle);
    std::string getjobtitle() const;
    void formatprint() override;
};

Employee::Employee() : Person(), jobtitle{ "The Default Role" }
{}

Employee::Employee(const std::string& aname, int argage, const
std::string& ajobtitle) : Person(aname, argage), jobtitle{ ajobtitle }
{}

Employee::Employee(const Employee& rhs) : Person(rhs), jobtitle{ rhs.
jobtitle }
{
}

Employee& Employee::operator=(const Employee& rhs)
{
    Person::operator=(rhs);
    jobtitle = rhs.jobtitle;
    return *this;
}
```

```
Employee::Employee(Employee&& rhs) noexcept : Person(std::move(rhs)),
jobtitle{ std::move(rhs.jobtitle) }
{
}

Employee& Employee::operator=(Employee&& rhs) noexcept
{
    Person::operator=(std::move(rhs));
    jobtitle = std::move(rhs.jobtitle);
    return *this;
}

void Employee::setjobtitle(const std::string& ajobtitle)
{
    jobtitle = ajobtitle;
}

std::string Employee::getjobtitle() const
{
    return jobtitle;
}

void Employee::formatprint()
{
    std::cout << "Employee's name: " << getname() << ", age: "
    << getage() << ", job title: " << jobtitle << '\n';
}
}

using namespace nm;

int main()
{
    // a vector unique pointers
    std::vector<std::unique_ptr<Person>> v2;
    v2.emplace_back(std::make_unique<Employee>("Sample Name 1", 20,
    "Developer"));
```

```
v2.emplace_back(std::make_unique<Employee>("Sample Name 2", 25,
"Engineer"));
v2.emplace_back(std::make_unique<Employee>("Sample Name 3", 30,
"Quality Assurance"));
v2.emplace_back(std::make_unique<Employee>("Sample Name 4", 35,
"Human Resources"));
v2.emplace_back(std::make_unique<Employee>("Sample Name 5", 40,
"Manager"));
v2.emplace_back(std::make_unique<Employee>("Sample Name 6", 45,
"CEO"));
for (const auto& el : v2)
{
    el->formatprint();
}

std::cout << "Testing..." << '\n';
// testing
Employee o3; // The default constructor invoked
Employee o4("Sample name 7", 50, "Accountant");
// copy assignment test:
o3 = o4;
o3.formatprint();
}
```

Output:

```
Employee's name: Sample Name 1, age: 20, job title: Developer
Employee's name: Sample Name 2, age: 25, job title: Engineer
Employee's name: Sample Name 3, age: 30, job title: Quality Assurance
Employee's name: Sample Name 4, age: 35, job title: Human Resources
Employee's name: Sample Name 5, age: 40, job title: Manager
Employee's name: Sample Name 6, age: 45, job title: CEO
Testing...
Employee's name: Sample name 7, age: 50, job title: Accountant
```

In our `main` function, we create a vector of unique pointers of `Persons` and add instances of type `Employee`, thus creating a vector of polymorphic objects/pointers. As an alternative to the `push_back` member function, we used the more efficient `emplace_back` member function to insert new objects into a container. Both options are viable.

Then using the range-based for loop, we iterate through a vector of pointers and invoke the overridden function `formatprint` using the `->` operator.

Please note that most of the time, we want a vector of objects, not a vector of pointers. But this is one of those rare situations where we indeed want a vector of pointers to maintain a collection of polymorphic objects.

Finally, in the last few statements, we add a simple test demonstrating the use of a copy assignment operator. This concludes our fifth project.

Project VI: Information System – Multiple Files

Write a program that splits the code from *Project V* into multiple (source and header) files. Additional requirements:

- Put the `Person` class declaration inside a *person.h* header file. Implement header guards.

- Put the `Employee` class declaration inside an *employee.h* header file. Implement header guards.

- Put the `Person` class definition inside a *person.cpp* source file. Include the *person.h* header file into a *person.cpp* source file.

- Put the `Employee` class definition inside an *employee.cpp* source file. Include the *employee.h* header file into a *person.cpp* source file.

- In the main program file called *source.cpp*, include the *employee.h* header file and create a vector of polymorphic objects.

- Include additional header files where appropriate.

- Wrap the classes' code inside a namespace `nm`.

- Compile all the source files and run the program.

Now, we have five different files in total. We have two header files, called *person.h* and *employee.h*, and three source files, called *person.cpp*, *employee.cpp*, and *source.cpp*. The basic project skeleton with the code guards now looks like this:

person.h:

```
#ifndef PERSON_H
#define PERSON_H

#include <string>
#include <iostream>

namespace nm
{

}

#endif // !PERSON_H
```

employee.h:

```
#ifndef EMPLOYEE_H
#define EMPLOYEE_H

#include "person.h"

namespace nm
{

}

#endif // !EMPLOYEE_H
```

person.cpp:

```
#include "person.h"

namespace nm
{

}
```

employee.cpp:

```cpp
#include "employee.h"

namespace nm
{

}
```

source.cpp:

```cpp
#include "employee.h"
#include <vector>
#include <memory>

using namespace nm;

int main()
{

}
```

Let us now add the Person base class declaration to a *person.h* file. Listing: *person.h*:

```cpp
#ifndef PERSON_H
#define PERSON_H

#include <string>
#include <iostream>

namespace nm
{
    // base class Person
    class Person
    {
    private:
        std::string name;
        int age;
    public:
        // default constructor
        Person();
```

```cpp
        // user-provided constructor
        Person(const std::string& aname, int argage);
        // copy constructor
        Person(const Person& rhs);
        // copy assignment operator
        Person& operator=(const Person& rhs);
        // move constructor
        Person(Person&& rhs) noexcept;
        // move assignment operator
        Person& operator=(Person&& rhs) noexcept;
        void printname();
        void printage();
        void printdata();
        std::string getname() const;
        int getage() const;
        void setname(const std::string& aname);
        void setage(int argage);
        virtual void formatprint();
        // virtual base class destructor
        virtual ~Person() {}
    };
}

#endif // !PERSON_H
```

Let us add the Person class definition to a *person.cpp* file. Listing: *person.cpp*:

```cpp
#include "person.h"

namespace nm
{
    Person::Person() : name{ "Default name" }, age{ -1 }
    {
    }
```

```cpp
Person::Person(const std::string& aname, int argage) : name{ aname },
age{ argage }
{
}

Person::Person(const Person& rhs) : name{ rhs.name }, age{ rhs.age }
{
}

Person& Person::operator=(const Person& rhs)
{
    name = rhs.name;
    age = rhs.age;
    return *this;
}

Person::Person(Person&& rhs) noexcept : name{ std::move(rhs.name) },
age{ std::move(rhs.age) }
{
}

Person& Person::operator=(Person&& rhs) noexcept
{
    name = std::move(name);
    age = std::move(age);
    return *this;
}

void Person::printname()
{
    std::cout << name << '\n';
}

void Person::printage()
{
    std::cout << age << '\n';
}
```

```cpp
void Person::printdata()
{
    std::cout << name << ' ' << age << '\n';
}

std::string Person::getname() const
{
    return name;
}

int Person::getage() const
{
    return age;
}

void Person::setname(const std::string& aname)
{
    name = aname;
}

void Person::setage(int argage)
{
    age = argage;
}

void Person::formatprint()
{
    std::cout << "Person's name: " << name << ", age: " << age << '\n';
}
}
```

The Employee derived class declaration goes into an *employee.h* file. Listing: *employee.h*:

```cpp
#ifndef EMPLOYEE_H
#define EMPLOYEE_H

#include "person.h"
```

```cpp
namespace nm
{
    // derived class Employee
    class Employee : public Person
    {
    private:
        std::string jobtitle;
    public:
        // default constructor
        Employee();
        // user provided constructor
        Employee(const std::string& aname, int argage, const std::string&
        ajobtitle);
        // copy constructor
        Employee(const Employee& rhs);
        // copy assignment operator
        Employee& operator=(const Employee& rhs);
        // move constructor
        Employee(Employee&& rhs) noexcept;
        // move assignment operator
        Employee& operator=(Employee&& rhs) noexcept;
        void setjobtitle(const std::string& ajobtitle);
        std::string getjobtitle() const;
        void formatprint() override;
    };
}

#endif // !EMPLOYEE_H
```

The definition of the Employee class goes inside the *employee.cpp* file. Listing: *employee.cpp*:

```cpp
#include "employee.h"

namespace nm
{
    Employee::Employee() : Person(), jobtitle{"The Default Role"}
    {}
```

```
Employee::Employee(const std::string& aname, int argage, const
std::string& ajobtitle) : Person(aname, argage), jobtitle{ ajobtitle }
{}

Employee::Employee(const Employee& rhs) : Person(rhs), jobtitle{
rhs.jobtitle }
{
}

Employee& Employee::operator=(const Employee& rhs)
{
    Person::operator=(rhs);
    jobtitle = rhs.jobtitle;
    return *this;
}

Employee::Employee(Employee&& rhs) noexcept : Person(std::move(rhs)),
jobtitle{ std::move(rhs.jobtitle) }
{
}

Employee& Employee::operator=(Employee&& rhs) noexcept
{
    Person::operator=(std::move(rhs));
    jobtitle = std::move(rhs.jobtitle);
    return *this;
}

void Employee::setjobtitle(const std::string& ajobtitle)
{
    jobtitle = ajobtitle;
}

std::string Employee::getjobtitle() const
{
    return jobtitle;
}
```

```cpp
    void Employee::formatprint()
    {
        std::cout << "Employee's name: " << getname() << ", age: "
        << getage() << ", job title: " << jobtitle << '\n';
    }
}
```

Finally, we populate the function main with the remaining source code from *Project V*. Listing:

source.cpp:

```cpp
#include "employee.h"
#include <vector>
#include <memory>

using namespace nm;

int main()
{
    // a vector of unique pointers
    std::vector<std::unique_ptr<Person>> v2;
    v2.emplace_back(std::make_unique<Employee>("Sample Name 1", 20,
    "Developer"));
    v2.emplace_back(std::make_unique<Employee>("Sample Name 2", 25,
    "Engineer"));
    v2.emplace_back(std::make_unique<Employee>("Sample Name 3", 30,
    "Quality Assurance"));
    v2.emplace_back(std::make_unique<Employee>("Sample Name 4", 35, "Human
    Resources"));
    v2.emplace_back(std::make_unique<Employee>("Sample Name 5", 40,
    "Manager"));
    v2.emplace_back(std::make_unique<Employee>("Sample Name 6", 45,
    "CEO"));
    for (const auto& el : v2)
    {
        el->formatprint();
    }
```

```
    std::cout << "Testing..." << '\n';
    // testing
    Employee o3; // The default constructor invoked
    Employee o4("Sample name 7", 50, "Accountant");
    // copy assignment test:
    o3 = o4;
    o3.formatprint();
}
```

In this project, we had two classes, a base class Person and a derived class Employee. We put the Person class declaration into a *person.h* header file, and the definition goes into a *person.cpp* file.

For a derived class Employee, the declaration goes into an *employee.h* header file, and the implementation goes into the *employee.cpp* source file. The main program is located inside the *source.cpp* file. Finally, we compile all the source files together using the following command if on Linux:

```
g++ -Wall -std=c++17 person.cpp employee.cpp source.cpp
```

We then run the program:

```
./a.out
```

And observe the results:

Output:

```
Employee's name: Sample Name 1, age: 20, job title: Developer
Employee's name: Sample Name 2, age: 25, job title: Engineer
Employee's name: Sample Name 3, age: 30, job title: Quality Assurance
Employee's name: Sample Name 4, age: 35, job title: Human Resources
Employee's name: Sample Name 5, age: 40, job title: Manager
Employee's name: Sample Name 6, age: 45, job title: CEO
Testing...
Employee's name: Sample name 7, age: 50, job title: Accountant
```

The output is the same as with *Project V*, but now we better organize our code by splitting multiple declarations into header files and multiple definitions into appropriate source files. We also learned how to better logically manage the code by wrapping classes and other entities in a namespace.

Index

A

Array definition
  char, int, and double objects, 59
  elements, 53
  pointer, 54
  reference type, 54
  single character, 57
  standard input, 55
  strings, 55
  substring, 56, 58
Arrays
  char declaration, 35
  elements, 35
  implicit conversions, 199
  initialization, 35
Automatic storage duration
  stack memory, 102
  variables, 105, 107
Automatic type deduction
  constant type, 52
  initialization, 51
  reference type, 51

B

Book inventory
  arguments, 351, 352
  class declaration, 363
  compilation string, 366
  constructor, 348, 350, 352
  getpages() method, 354–357, 359
  information system, 392–432

  message logger, 367–385
  printdata() member function, 359–361
  requirements, 347, 362
  source and header files,
    362–367, 386–392
  source.cpp file, 347
  source/header files, 362
  title method, 348

C

C++11 standards
  automatic type deduction, 282
  concurrency
    command line, 294
    executable file, 294
    locking/unlocking mutexes,
      299, 300
    parameters, 295
    threads, 294–299
  constexpr specifier, 285
  definition, 281
  delete/default functions, 301–304
  erase() member function, 289
  features, 281
  initializer lists, 283
  insert() member function, 288, 291
  Lambda expressions, 284
  move semantics, 284
  range-based loops, 282
  rvalue reference, 284
  scoped enumerators, 286

© Slobodan Dmitrović 2023
S. Dmitrović, *Modern C++ for Absolute Beginners*, https://doi.org/10.1007/978-1-4842-9274-7

F, G

H

I, J, K

Printed in the United States
by Baker & Taylor Publisher Services